walking in wonder

walking in wonder

RESILIENCE IN MINISTRY

George R. Sinclair, Jr.

CASCADE *Books* • Eugene, Oregon

WALKING IN WONDER
Resilience in Ministry

Copyright © 2014 George R. Sinclair, Jr. All rights reserved. Except for brief quotations in critical publications or reviews, no part of this book may be reproduced in any manner without prior written permission from the publisher. Write: Permissions, Wipf and Stock Publishers, 199 W. 8th Ave., Suite 3, Eugene, OR 97401.

Cascade Books
An Imprint of Wipf and Stock Publishers
199 W. 8th Ave., Suite 3
Eugene, OR 97401
www.wipfandstock.com

ISBN 13: 978-1-62654-374-2

Cataloging-in-Publication data:

Sinclair, George R., Jr.

Walking in wonder : resilience in ministry / George R. Sinclair, Jr.

xvi + 108 p.; 23 cm—Includes bibliographical references.

ISBN 13: 978-1-62654-374-2

1. Christian leadership. 2. Pastoral theology. 3. Presbyterian Church—Clergy—Anecdotes. I. Title.

BV4011 S49 2014

Manufactured in the USA.

Table of Contents

Foreword by Michael Jinkins vii
Acknowledgments xi
Preface xiii

CHAPTER ONE: Wonder: Enchanted by Awesome Mystery 1
CHAPTER TWO: Acedia and Grace-Tempered Pride 14
CHAPTER THREE: Hubris and the Gift of Humility 27
CHAPTER FOUR: Hope, Enduring Fragility, and Failure 40
CHAPTER FIVE: Steadfast Love, Reframing Ambiguity 54
CHAPTER SIX: Leading: It's About You 68
CHAPTER SEVEN: Following: It's Not About You 81
CHAPTER EIGHT: Resilience: A Christ-Shaped Life of Freedom 94

Bibliography 107

Foreword

by Michael Jinkins

"Do you not know?
  Have you not heard?
The Lord is the everlasting God,
  The Creator of the ends of the earth.
He will not grow tired or weary,
  And his understanding no one can fathom.
He gives strength to the weary
  And increases the power of the weak.
Even youths grow tired and weary,
  And young men stumble and fall;
But those who hope in the Lord
  Will renew their strength.
They will soar on wings like eagles;
  They will run and not grow weary,
  They will walk and not be faint."
    (Isa 40: 28–31 NIV)

MINISTRY IS A SPIRITUAL discipline. Ministry is, of course, much more than this, but it is never less. Those people who take vows to enter into Christian ministry (and I would include in this the whole people of God or the entire "*laos*" of God, the so-called "laity" as well as those ordained to various ministries) are promising to live their lives with a particular orientation, a spiritual orientation, an orientation toward God that in and of itself points to the reality at the heart of all human life. We depend upon an Other for all of life. As Saint Paul reminds us, drawing on the ancient wisdom of Stoicism: in God "we live and move and have our being" (Acts 17:28). And ministry orients us toward this dependence, this reliance, which is grounded in a consciousness of God's trustworthiness.

This is not an abstract philosophical idea. No, indeed; this is the life-giving core of all faith.

Every breath we draw is a gift of God. Every moment we enjoy is ours at the pleasure of God. The Source of all we are, all we know, all we feel, and all we do is the God who creates us not because God needs us, but from God's overabundance of love. And this Source of all is not removed from us by millions of years of history or millions of light-years of space. Nor is this Source merely shrouded among the hazy folds of legend. As the late Hans Urs von Balthasar said so eloquently: "Herein lies the most unfathomable aspect of the Mystery of God: that what is absolutely primal is no statically self-contained and comprehensible reality, but one that exists solely in dispensing itself: a flowing wellspring with no holding-trough beneath it."[1] The Source of all, the Divine Whence from which all life proceeds, holds us in existence from one moment to the next, breathing into us what we need to live and move. The ministries in which we are engaged and the ministers we are called to be tell this story with every act of mercy and grace, with every expression of love and life. We are called into the divine reality to draw our breath from the breath of God. Breath is for sharing, not for holding. Inhaling, exhaling. Such is the rhythm of life and of ministry.

This is something of the theological backdrop behind the crucial question with which George Sinclair opens this book. "What keeps you walking in faithful ministry?" he asks. "What makes it possible to keep on keeping on, over the long haul of life and faith and hope and love?" And, he implies also, "What makes you stumble?" God is, as von Balthasar said, "a flowing wellspring with no holding-trough beneath it," but we are not God. We depend upon another for that strength to keep on keeping on, or, to borrow the language of Isaiah, to "walk and not faint."

Recent research has confirmed what many intuitively have believed: that long-term success in life and leadership—as opposed to the "flash-in-the-pan" variety of success—depends in large measure on one's internal capacities to persist even against great odds and opposition. The late Rabbi Edwin Friedman observed that success, particularly in leadership, requires "persistence in the face of resistance and downright rejection," "a kind of

---

1. Von Balthasar, *Credo*, 30.

relentless drive."[2] But such persistence alone can become brittle, hard, and rigid. Persistence can be a very inhumane quality, a capacity that, as Friedman himself observed, "borders on the demonic."[3] How can those in ministry cultivate a quality of persistence that reflects the grace and love of God? How can those in ministry cultivate a quality of leadership that reflects this grace and love of God in such a way that others are drawn to share in this grace and love? How can those in ministry cultivate a quality of life that feeds and nurtures all they do and all they are?

With a rare combination of gifts pastoral and scholarly, Dr. Sinclair explores what it takes to flourish in ministry. He draws on biblical and theological resources, but he is also conversant with the literature of leadership, organizational behavior, and management. He moves with ease from popular resources such as Andrew Zolli's work on resilience to theologians such as Jürgen Moltmann. To say that his understandings are biblically informed is an understatement. He breathes a biblical ethos with ease, reflecting his deep familiarity with the Old and New Testaments. Reading Sinclair is like engaging in a riveting conversation with a pastor and colleague who possesses a remarkably nimble mind, a deep faith in God, and a love for good books and fascinating ideas. But his conversation never simply meanders and is never satisfied with pursuing idle speculations. Again and again, he takes us, first from one angle and then from another, into a deeper understanding of what it means to find in the God of infinite love and wonder the inexhaustible Source for our own lives and ministries.

The stories he tells, drawn from experience, are fresh and illuminating. The insights he provides cut close to home. The chapters that follow offer opportunities for everyone who is engaged in ministry to reflect and to grow. "What keeps you walking in faithful ministry?" Dr. Sinclair asks. With the patience and wisdom of a great pastor, he opens to us that enduring Word, which is always prophetic and priestly, reminding us that God alone makes it possible not only to run a sprint or soar above the clouds, but to walk and to keep on walking the long, long road of discipleship to which Christ calls us.

---

2. Friedman, *A Failure of Nerve*, 188.
3. Ibid.

Acknowledgments

A FRIEND ONCE ASKED if I thought I had a book in me. "Maybe," I shrugged, "I don't know; we'll see." I want to thank Ted Beason for planting that seed over twenty years ago. I also want to thank President Michael Jinkins and Dean Susan Garrett of Louisville Presbyterian Theological Seminary, whose encouragement, advice, and involvement gave roots to this project.

During a conference at LPTS, I told Michael about Ted's question. Michael, always energetic and curious, brightly asked, "What are you going to write about?" I answered, "I know about ministry but I don't want to write a book about survival or practice. I want to think theologically about ministry. Ministry takes a toll and without deeper resources we wither and perish."

"I think you're on to something," Michael said, stopping us midway across the sunlit quad. "Ministry is a fight. We get knocked down and we have to get back up, again and again. Talk to Susan; she'll help you, we both will." And they did.

The next day I woke up with a title and table of contents in my head. I'd like to thank Bill Brown of Columbia Theological Seminary whose book, *The Seven Pillars of Creation: The Bible, Science, and the Ecology of Wonder*, prompted me to consider the category of wonder. Pairing it with resilience came out of the blue; John Mulder helped me get it on the ground. I am deeply grateful for his wisdom and encouragement throughout this journey.

A number of colleagues read early drafts. Three deserve special mention: Steven Kurtz, Al Reese, and Kathryn Threadgill. Thanks for your friendship and helping me to see things I could not see alone. Likewise, I am indebted to the communion of saints where I currently serve and to those before them who took me in as their pastor. Without the people of God this book would not have been written.

ACKNOWLEDGMENTS

Wipf and Stock Publishers have been a pleasure to work with. Thank you for sticking your neck out on a previously unpublished writer. And thank you, Rodney Clapp, for making my prose far more readable and precise. Whatever errors that remain are my own.

Lastly, I want to thank my family. My daughter, Meredith, Assistant Professor of Secondary English Education at Southern Connecticut State University, not only helped her father's English but also formatted the book. My son, Sean, helped keep me in good humor and told me I could do it. This book is dedicated to my wife, Paula, whose resiliency has inspired me for forty years. Thank you for loving me and walking this path hand in hand.

In the stories I tell, names have been changed or accounts fictionalized in view of confidentially, with the exceptions of those publically known or cited.

Preface

WHAT KEEPS YOU WALKING in faithful ministry? What keeps you walking when you've forgotten the Name of the One who called you? Or maybe you know the Name but the Name no longer quickens your pace or your heart? What keeps you walking when you long for God but all you feel is distant, empty space? What keeps you walking when you stumble and fall because of your ego or stupidity or sin? What keeps you walking when you are knocked down or run over or defeated? What keeps you walking when you are disappointed or rejected or worn out? What keeps you walking when you don't know what to do next? What keeps you walking when the lump in your throat won't go away and it's not because you are hopeful but because you are terrified? What keeps you walking when you must lead and you'd rather duck and run? What keeps you walking when you are not the center of attention but simply one in a great cloud of witnesses? What keeps you walking when you have a cross to bear but lack freedom or courage to carry it?

I have a modest proposal: walk in wonder enchanted by the awesome mystery of God and you will keep walking. You will grow resilient. Resilience in ministry is born of wonder when we bow before the awesome mystery of God and follow.

Ministers are called to be "stewards of God's mysteries" (1 Cor 4:1). Stewards don't get behind mystery in order to explain it or package it or broker it. Stewards are witnesses. They give testimony. While testimony may involve puzzle solving or simply "puzzling," as a colleague aptly suggests, testimony does not lead to fixed, flat explanations but rather to love in motion, to wondrous love. The difference is the difference between idolatry and worship.

So, how do we walk in wonder? First, lose the notion that God can be comprehended. Faith seeks understanding, not comprehension. Second,

PREFACE

expect to be surprised, dumbfounded, decentered, rearranged; in short, expect to be awed. Third, learn to play or otherwise take yourself less seriously so you may take God more seriously. God actually shows up even when we're not around! Fourth, expect to suffer. If you are fully engaged with the Crucified, you will suffer. Lastly, expect to find joy beyond belief, joy that sometimes is just plain silliness and laughter and at other times the kind that takes your breath away. That's the short version of my proposal, now a slightly longer one.

The Emmaus Road

I have a hunch—no—a confession: most days I don't live with a perpetual sense of wonder. I am not routinely enchanted. Yes, there are moments of exhilaration, surprise, glimpses of the kingdom come, but most days pass without noteworthy occurrence. As Daniel Kahneman wryly observes, I walk through most days thinking that "what I see is all there is."[1]

I readily identify with Luke's stories of Easter. Think about it—the women don't go to the tomb expecting to meet or see Jesus. They return to complete his burial, which is why they are "perplexed" when they don't find him. It's also why they are "terrified" when the "two men in dazzling clothes" suddenly appear suggesting that they're looking in the wrong place (Luke 24:1–5). They should be among the living, not the dead.

Wonder doesn't come naturally. We're more likely shocked into it. We resist wonder. Consider the disciples' response when the women return from the tomb and report to them: "these words seemed to them an idle tale, and *they did not believe* them" (Luke 24:11; emphasis mine). So much for a natural disposition or constant state of wonder. The disciples don't believe. Okay, give Peter credit. He at least runs to the tomb, looks in, and is "amazed"—not quite faith, but a step in that direction.

Awe is not our default condition. Consider the two disciples who leave Jerusalem by way of the Emmaus Road. They "had hoped" Jesus was "the one to redeem Israel." Notice the past tense. If they once hoped, they did so no longer. The two can recite the creed. They know the catechism: "Jesus of Nazareth . . . was a prophet mighty in deed and word before God and all the people . . . he was handed over to be condemned to death and crucified" (Luke 24:19–20). The two know the story but not the Storyteller. They even know that some said he was alive but they had "not seen him."

1. Kahneman, *Thinking, Fast and Slow*, 85.

PREFACE

Readers of Luke of course know Jesus is standing right there in front of the disciples, if they will just open their eyes. But "eye-opening" requires the mysterious work of God. Like the disciples, we must wait for the Stranger to "interpret" the Scriptures and be "made known" in "the breaking of the bread." And even then, even then the Presence is illusive. As soon as the eyes of the two travelers are opened, as soon as they recognize the Lord he "vanishes." Why must he "vanish"? Why does he not stay the night? Perhaps this is Luke's device to move the plot along, but more likely it is because Luke understands that God is not comprehended. God is never "fully grasped." Hearts burn, yes; eyes are opened; the disciples are sent and know the Presence in the broken bread; but God is not contained, possessed, controlled.

Consider again the final Easter evening meeting. The travelers leave Emmaus and return to Jerusalem. Their story spills out. The disciples were all ears when "Jesus himself stood among them and greeted them, 'Peace be with you'" (Luke 24:36). People accustomed to God appearing should hardly be "startled" or "terrified" when God shows up. People who know the creed should know better than to think they are "seeing a ghost" when it is the Lord. But such was the first Easter and, I would argue, every Easter. If God were obvious, as plain as the nose on our face, we would never be startled or terrified. And we'd also never have anything called faith or hope or love. Wonder is not our default mode of being. We are more likely to be shocked into it, surprised, or, as with the first disciples, "disbelieving with joy" when the One in our midst asks of us, "Have you anything here to eat?" (Luke 24:41).

This book is written out of a conviction that God supplies daily bread—wondrous love that keeps us walking in faithfulness. Chapter 1 will explore the relationship between wonder and enchantment. How do we keep walking unless we are enchanted? These concepts are foundational for all that follows.

Acedia and hubris are constant tempting companions to ministry. In chapters 2 and 3 I will visit these two deadly sins and entertain the conviction that enchantment with the awesome mystery of God offers an antidote to both: grace tempered pride and the gift of humility. Without either we wilt and/or lapse into idolatry.

Every leader is circumscribed by limits: institutional, social, cultural, physical, spiritual, personal, or more pointedly—our humanity. How do we bounce back? Chapter 4 will address fragility and failure through the lens of resilient hope.

When leaders are fearful, when churches or individuals or families are fearful, when organizations react out of fear, they spiral in dysfunction or sometimes simply act badly. Ambiguity in ministry is unavoidable. In chapter 5 I will ask how God's steadfast love reframes ambiguity when we follow the One who is at work far beyond what we ask or imagine. How do leaders walk in God's steadfast love?

When self-awareness is absent, leadership is impossible. Leaders must show up. They cannot disappear. In chapters 6 and 7 I will argue that leaders must, may, and can show up when they realize that more is at stake than their own determination, creativity, skill, or practiced wisdom. To lead we must follow.

Pastors and other leaders begin work equipped with mental maps, skill sets, character strengths, and no small measure of hope. No matter how well equipped or personally determined, pastors and other leaders face not just single, occasional difficulties and discouragement but long years of difficulties and discouragement. Those long years take a toll. Any pastor who has ever held the hand of parents at the grave of a newborn, any pastor who has ever fought with a board over a complex social or institutional problem, or raised money in a culture of scarcity, realizes that patient endurance draws upon and at times exhausts creativity, physical stamina, and spiritual resources. In my concluding chapter I hope to make a case for resilience when we bear witness to the awesome mystery of the triune God who asks us, "Have you anything here to eat?" When we walk in wonder and are paused by the awesome mystery of the triune God, our answer will be a resounding and joyful "Yes."

CHAPTER ONE

Wonder: Enchanted by Awesome Mystery

Density

HAVE YOU EVER EXPERIENCED the holy? When was the last time you experienced the holy? What did you experience?

I have been asking these questions a lot lately, not only of others but myself. Here is some of the testimony I have heard.

I experienced the holy when my child was born.

I experienced the holy when I was delivered from addiction to prescription pain medication.

I experienced the holy when my daughter was married.

I experienced the holy when I watched the sun come up on a clear morning at the beach.

I experienced the holy when I witnessed the changing of the guard at the Tomb of the Unknown Soldier in Arlington National Cemetery.

I experienced the holy at a graveside service when a mother of triplets born three months prematurely knelt and gently placed her hand on the small coffin of the four-month-old she and her husband had named Madeline. Seven months later, I experienced the holy when Madeline's parents stood before a baptismal font for the baptism of Maddie's siblings.

I experienced the holy when I held the leathery hand of an eighty-six-year-old woman as the sister she had long cared for lay dying in the next room.

I experienced the holy when a sixty-year-old shared the pain and sorrow of her brother's suicide while thanking her church for the care and support she and her family had received.

I experienced the holy when two men, alienated by hard feelings of misunderstanding, spoke in hushed tones of embrace on a quiet Sunday morning before worship.

I experienced the holy when a twenty-eight-year-old homeless man asked me to pray for him. I was just going to give him bus fare and leave. He asked me to pray.

I experienced the holy when . . .

How would you complete the sentence?

Asking about the holy is a bit like asking about gravity. We don't notice gravity unless we are riding a roller coaster or pushing a child on a swing. Gravity just is. We don't have to think about it or believe in it for it to exist. Aside from particle physicists, most of us don't go through our day considering the forces of nature. We don't have to understand equations defining the interactions of strong force and weak force and electromagnetism and gravity to borrow a cup of sugar. We just walk across the street and hope our neighbor is not only home but generous. To borrow sugar, we don't have to understand that above a temperature of a million billion Kelvin the four forces of nature merge again into one—or so it is theorized. Sugar borrowers (and lenders for that matter) don't have to understand the Grand Unified Theory to bake birthday cakes.

Experiences of the holy are like that—they don't require a specialist's knowledge. You don't have to be a theologian or biblical scholar or even consider yourself religious or spiritual to be enchanted—you need only be alive and notice the silence, a silence that is always speaking: "the voice of the Lord is over the waters" (Ps 29:3). Notice may be faint and inchoate or loud and clear. Enchantment is not singular except that we are drawn, pulled, fascinated, and sometimes undone or made still. The voice "over the waters" speaks.

My wife teaches eighth grade Honors Algebra I. When the first semester begins, she teaches a lesson on the definition of the density of rational numbers: *between any two rational numbers there exists an infinite number of other rational numbers.* When teaching this concept, my wife says something extraordinary unfolds in her classroom. While most of her students may remember a lesson about population density or the density of water molecules, few if any have ever considered number density until my wife talks about something middle school students love—pizza!

Before talking about pizza, my wife draws a number line on her smart board, marking zero and one-half. She then asks her students to name the fraction that comes exactly between zero and one-half.

"That's easy; 1/4," they say.

"Okay, what number is exactly between 0 and 1/4?"

"1/8," they answer.

"How about between 0 and 1/8?"

"1/16."

"How about between 0 and 1/16?"

"1/32."

"How about between 0 and 1/32?"

"1/64."

About this time (and sometimes the fractions run to 1/128 or 1/256 depending on her play and her students' reactions) my wife asks, "How long can we keep dividing by two before we reach zero?" Puzzled looks appear, consternation, a few I-don't-know frowns, but also, usually, cautious guesses, "Forever?" To which my wife replies, "Well, then, can we ever get to zero?" Again, puzzled frowns appear, along with a few eyes glimmering hints of recognition. That's when Paula, the math teacher, delivers her imaginary pizza pie.

"Imagine you order a freshly baked pepperoni pizza but the maker forgot to slice it. Nobody wants to eat a whole pizza (okay some of you), but even if you want the whole pizza you will likely make right-sized pieces first. Say, you cut the pizza in half, give one half away and keep the other for yourself. That's still a big slice of pizza so you cut it again and since you are feeling generous you give the other away. Now you have a quarter-slice. It's still too big to handle so you cut it again, give half to your friend, and are left with a normal size single serving. Maybe you're at a party. Your friends are there. You don't want anyone left out. You cut your single serving in half again, give one piece away and keep the other for yourself. By now you have a pretty small piece of pizza, just a bite. Could you cut your bite-size pizza again? By this time some students begin waving excited hands, "Are you saying, Mrs. Sinclair, that we could keep on slicing that pizza forever?"

"That's what I'm saying, which is why if you keep on slicing it, which everybody knows is physically impossible, about all you would have left is the smell of pepperoni. Nobody does that but theoretically you could slice your pizza forever, which is also why we never reach zero on our number line when dividing rational numbers by two."

"That's awesome, Mrs. Sinclair. I get it; *between any two rational numbers there exists an infinite number of other rational numbers.*" Density.

Furrowed brows relax. Imagination is released; a pattern previously hidden is seen; something resembling light turns on. Call it wonder.

"How about some pi?" the teacher asks. "And I am not talking pizza."

"Mrs. Sinclair," I don't even like math but this is my favorite class. I think I'd like some pi." The students are all ears. They are enchanted. They want more.

What would ministry become, how would it be different, if we lived with a greater sense of wonder, if we were more routinely "enchanted"? In part, I think we would take ourselves less seriously and God more seriously. And in the process, not only would life become far more interesting, we would grow far more resilient. We might learn to dance and sing or throw ourselves more fully into the song and dance life is. Before concluding that this sober, left-brain Presbyterian has taken leave of his senses, let me offer a caution: don't add "wonder" to your to-do list. "Now I must not only work professionally with faith, hope, and love; I must have WONDER!" Not so fast. Yes, wonder may be a disposition, but before anything else wonder is a response.

Enchantment

Charles Taylor argues that we live in a disenchanted world. We no longer expect reality to impose meaning. Reality, we presume, is created or projected by our minds. In an enchanted world "charged" objects impose meaning.[1] Today, we see the world differently. We define it. We "charge" it with meaning. We don't expect the voice over the waters to define us; we define it, or, as Taylor puts it, we are "buffered."[2] The buffered self disengages from everything outside the mind. Ultimate purposes are created by us.

Taylor contrasts the buffered self with the porous self.[3] The porous self, says Taylor, is "vulnerable." As my wife's eighth grade Algebra students demonstrate, we are gifted, despite buffering, with a porous nature. We can, when sufficiently paused, hear the "voice over the waters." We may

1. Taylor, *A Secular Age*, 35.
2. Ibid., 27.
3. Ibid.

be enchanted. Apart from enchantment, discovery is impossible. Reality imposes itself. It speaks. The world is knowable not because we are knowledgeable but because the silence speaks. When we name reality (whether defining the density of rational numbers or puzzling over the Grand Unified Theory) we do so because reality has spoken. We don't create the voice; the voice creates us. Our calling is to name the voice as the voice wishes to be heard.

I believe four things...

"No one has ever seen God" (1 John 4:12).

"Although you have not seen God, you love God" (1 Pet 1:8).

"We love because God first loved us" (1 John 4:19).

"Those who do not love a brother or sister whom they have seen, cannot love God whom they have not seen" (1 John 4:20).

Ministers, no less than others, are susceptible to disenchantment. We may be "buffered." In that regard, we are no different than the first disciples. They didn't expect Jesus to show up or ask for supper. Yes, they talked about what happened on the road to Emmaus and perhaps some even planned what they would do next. But they didn't expect Jesus. They were "buffered." Disenchantment is not just a twenty-first-century phenomenon. It may be more prevalent today because we live anonymously and indoors, or because we don't grow our own food, or because the trauma of birth and death is cushioned if not anesthetized by medical practices, or because we have explanations for everything under the sun including the sun itself, but our location in the twenty-first century is not the sole cause of buffering. Disenchantment resides in the nature of God—"no one has ever seen God."

Enchantment and disenchantment exist because God is not obvious. If God were obvious, none of us would ever be enchanted. We are not enchanted by what we see but by what we don't see; otherwise, we would never climb the next mountain to discover what is on the other side or puzzle over the Grand Unified Theory. God's holiness, the mystery of God's otherness, hides God from plain view. That same holiness or mystery draws us, pulls us, enchants us.

Disenchantment or buffering likewise resides in the nature of faith itself—"Although you have not seen God, you love God." It is not a given that we will love either God or others (a topic to be pursued in chapter 5). Love does not exist apart from the possibility of not-love, no more so than faith exists apart from the possibility of non-faith. In a like manner, enchantment does not exist apart from the possibility of disenchantment.

None of us lives a fully enchanted life. Enchantment comes and goes not only because God is hidden or holy or free but also because faith is not a steady state. We are "buffered," but every now and then, something greater, or Someone greater, intrudes and we are no longer the sole creators of meaning. We are acted upon. The buffered self is shattered (okay, sometimes just *cracked* a little) and we experience One standing in our midst we had not expected. Silence is broken. The voice over the waters is heard. Faith and love and wonder are created.

Let me return to a few examples of silence heard—experiences of the holy or enchantment that break through our otherwise buffered existence. As I narrate these episodes, I invite you to consider times in your life when you experienced the holy.

Frank and Mary

Frank and Mary, both thirty, have been happily married for four years. They decide to start a family. When the early pregnancy test comes back positive they make an appointment with an OB-GYN, who confirms on their first visit that they will have a baby in eight months. Happy phone calls are made to parents and close friends. The young couple begins thinking about names. They are having a girl. "Maybe we should name her Annette after your mother," Frank offers. "Maybe Sylvia," Mary counters. "She's your favorite aunt and I really like the name." The couple agrees to save naming for later. They will know when it comes to them.

A nursery is prepared, pretty in pink. Baby showers follow. A rocker is secured, along with a changing table, car seat, and more gear than will fit into a small moving van. They are ready. The day comes—contractions. Oh, the contractions. "Is this the real thing?" They phone the hospital and the nurse advises that they come in. The expectant parents make a few nervous phone calls, load the car with a previously packed suitcase and follow a well-mapped route flashed by their onboard GPS. Upon arrival, mother is admitted. The father paces. After three hours, labor stops; uh-oh, now what? "Sometimes this happens," the nurse explains. "We'll wait another hour and if nothing changes we are sending you home." Sure enough, labor doesn't resume.

Disappointed and apprehensive, the young couple packs up and returns home. Despite their anxiety they stop for burgers. They manage to laugh and phone waiting grandparents with their inconclusive news. One day goes by; then two, then three; and wham, the contractions begin again. This time around, Mary looks different. The drive seems much longer. "Oh no, here comes another one. Get me to the hospital!"

When Frank and Mary arrive, Frank circles the crowded lot before double parking. Mary could care less if they get towed. After a hurried check-in they are assigned to Delivery Room Six. One hour passes. Contractions are now two minutes apart. When the OB comes in a second time she leans over monitoring tapes with studied patience. She retakes Mary's blood pressure. She orders an ultrasound, reassuring Frank and Mary that it's just a precaution. "Your pressure is higher than we'd like and the baby shows signs of distress. We just want to be sure everything is all right." Frank, a medical supply salesman, is used to being in charge. Helplessness is foreign territory. Before the scan is over, Mary screams again. Frank bites his bottom lip and mutters a seldom practiced prayer.

Green-suited people come and go with purpose. The OB appears, says, "Mary, are you ready to have that baby?" The next thirty minutes fly by for Frank. They are an eternity for Mary. With one last push from Mary and a great sigh from Frank, a seven-pound-four-ounce baby girl enters the world. Frank had no idea there would be so much blood. With matted hair and trembling hands Mary cradles her newborn. Frank and Mary look at each other and in one voice announce to the room, "We're naming her Annette." Brushing aside her still wet hair, Frank leans over Mary, puts a cheek to hers and rests his hand on the receiving blanket swaddling his newly born child. He whispers that he will be right back. He's phoning their parents.

Frank finds a quiet corner and telephones. "Dad, we have a girl. I can't believe it. I've never seen anything like it." Frank paused, his voice catching, "Dad, I thought I was going to lose them. I mean, I did and I didn't. It was awful. For a while there, I just didn't know. Everything happened so fast. But they're okay. They're going to be fine. She's beautiful. They're beautiful. I can't tell you how lucky we are."

Jeremy

Jeremy showed up one morning just before Sunday school. He was carrying a backpack that looked as frazzled and tired as he did. We spoke briefly. I invited him to my class. Jeremy took a seat at the far end of a long table in the center of the classroom. When class members welcomed him he lowered his head. A young woman near his age also appeared. She introduced herself as Molly. When I asked if she was with Jeremy she said she had met him "a few days ago." Molly took a front seat at the opposite end of the table from Jeremy. Molly piped up several times during class discussion. Jeremy sat silently, thumbing through the text I had given him.

When the class ended, Jeremy asked if I had a minute. I suggested that if he waited until the 11:00 service ended, I would have more time. Jeremy agreed, picked up his backpack, and headed to the sanctuary. He sat close to the front but on a side aisle. Molly disappeared.

During worship, Jeremy did not stand with the congregation or sing when hymns were played. He stared straight ahead, shoulders slumped. After greeting worshipers at the front door, I made my way back through the sanctuary and found Jeremy waiting in the lobby where we had first met. He explained that he was from Mississippi, near Jackson, and needed help. I told him I couldn't do anything just yet but if he could come back in the morning I would see him around 9 a.m.

The next day, after finishing an eight o'clock Bible study, I met Jeremy, backpack in hand, standing in the lobby. No Molly. Jeremy wanted to know what I could do. He needed $19.28 for a photo ID. The ID was required by a local ministry designed to help people get back on their feet. "My mammaw kicked me out," Jeremy began. "I don't much blame her. I've been in lots of trouble—in and out of jail and up to no good. My daddy's a drunk and my mama don't care. I got nobody. If I could just get $19.28 and bus fare across town, I might have a chance. I think I could make it. I got no where's to go."

I went to the bookkeeper and got $30 from petty cash. When I handed the folded bills to Jeremy he brightened. I gave him directions to the bus stop and told him which road to take to reach the DMV and secure his photo ID. "Yeah," Jeremy said, "you know those drivers; they'll help you out."

"That's right," I said.

"Hey, you wouldn't mind praying for me, would ya?"

The thought had crossed my mind. Whatever reluctance I had vanished. For some reason, and I can't explain why, I put my hand on Jeremy's shoulder. I prayed for safe travels and courage to keep going. When I opened my eyes, Jeremy's face was streaked with tears. He turned for the door and looked back. A smile broke across his face, "Hey, bro, thanks. I'm going to make it. This time I'm going to make it."

I haven't seen Jeremy since that day. I don't know if he made it, but I do know that those brief moments in the church lobby were charged with something more than $30 and a pat on the back.

Awesome Mystery

When Frank's daughter was born a light was turned on. As with my wife's Algebra students, the switch happened "all at once." Something came over him. He was carried away. The moment was charged with a surplus of meaning. He didn't create the moment; the moment created him. The day Jeremy asked me to pray for him was a moment like that. I hadn't expected it. I can't explain what passed between us or exactly what I experienced, but I know or I knew that something more was going on, or something more was present than a pastor helping a homeless twenty-eight-year-old. God was present.

Of course, God is always present, we say. God is with us, in us, among us, but like gravity God is not always felt or experienced or known in the same way that we don't know or experience gravity until our stomach falls when the plane we're on suddenly drops. We generally live unaware of gravity. That doesn't mean it's not present, only that it's not experienced or noticed.

I am a Presbyterian. By disposition, I prefer a "decently ordered" world. But, as a Presbyterian, I'm convinced that reason alone cannot account for our "decently ordered" world. Reason points beyond itself. Rudolf Otto[4] named this "beyond," or our experience of it the *mysterium tremendum*, or awesome mystery. I have a nagging worry or fear that too often I leave too little room for any experience of awesome mystery. I don't think I'm alone in this.

I routinely hear pastors and others express a longing for something more than business as usual. And the "business" of leading a church can become just that, business. After all, we're professionals, right? We become proficient at making hospital calls, knowing just the right word to say at just the right time; we're all ears when experts tell us how we can improve the church if we just follow their exciting new template; we become skilled at conducting meetings, planning agendas, adapting to change; we work harder and smarter to preach better sermons—all of which may be

---

4. Otto, *The Idea of the Holy*.

necessary but ultimately unimportant if God is squeezed out, or, worse, if we operate as if God were ours to command.

When I was a child summer thunderstorms routinely triggered power outages. When the lights went out, we didn't sit in the dark; we lit candles. Sometimes my mother handed out flashlights and suggested that we play hide and seek. A dark house is a great place to play hide and seek. Sometimes, though, we sat quietly, listened to the rain, and waited for the next crash of thunder while counting down seconds to determine its distance. When the power returned and the TV flickered on, the mood quickly changed like when snow turns to rain. Now and then when the storms ended we asked if we could turn the lights back off and continue our play or talk in the dark, but it was never the same.

Wonder has a similar character—it's a response, not a permanent condition. Insisting that we live with more wonder is a bit like asking someone to laugh at a joke or telling yourself before a party that you must have a good time. Jokes, like parties, refuse manipulation. Wonder, likewise, is not something we fabricate. Wonder is received.

Why Wonder?

Why read a book about "wonder"? Good question. Here's my short answer: wonder is inspired by awesome mystery. Ministers and most anyone living in the twenty-first century could stand some of both—awe and mystery.

To ask or write about wonder begs a theological question: "What is God like?" Or better, "Who is God?" As a Christian and more particularly as a Presbyterian minister, I happily confess my faith in the triune God. I regularly and gladly baptize in the name of the Father, Son, and Holy Spirit. The holy name is not unimportant. I could say that I am using "awesome mystery" interchangeably with what I mean by Father, Son, and Holy Spirit but that is only partly true. It is only partly true because we cannot substitute an abstraction for a name and say they are the same. They are not. My aim is more like Luke's in Acts 17. Luke takes us to Athens, where Paul observes "how extremely religious" the Athenians are. The "unknown god" they worship and/or "grope after" and occasionally "find" is the God Paul "proclaims." Paul begins where the Athenians are. He may not leave them there, but he starts where they are. He acknowledges that they have some sense of the holy, that they recognize there is more to life than meets the eye.

WONDER: ENCHANTED BY AWESOME MYSTERY

Okay, so maybe that's just Luke's spin on Paul, but it doesn't seem far from the first two chapters of Romans, where Paul argues that Greeks are without "excuse" because "what can be known about God is plain to them, because God has *shown it* to them" (Rom 1:19–20; emphasis mine). I think both Luke and Paul make a case for walking-around-knowledge of God. We all have it. Awe and mystery, or awesome mystery, is a given of human existence because God *shows up*, because God desires to be known. Human beings, consequently, are explorers. We are curious. We are wonderers. And we are these things not only because God *shows up* but also because the world provokes our interest and our curiosity. As Michael Polanyi[5] argues, reality speaks, silently so, or tacitly.

We don't possess one kind of self for knowing the interesting natural world and a second, alternative self for knowing God or experiencing awesome mystery. Natural scientists and theologians may use different tools and language maps, but they share the same brain, the same humanity. And both disciplines, at the deepest levels, share a common trait: passionate intuition[6] inspired by awesome mystery.

Reality is "dense." And by *reality* I mean both God and the natural world. There is always more to be known than we know. I want to make a case for that, which in some ways is stating the obvious, but in our flattened-down-explanation-for-everything-managed world, even and especially the managed world called "church," we act as if we know it all, as if we are the sole creators of meaning. I want to make a case for wonder not only at the extremes of human experience, but at its center. Wonder is not peripheral to human existence, but central. Without it, we perish. Okay, that may be extreme, but we at the very least grow bored or arrogant, neither of which is congruent with the source or sources of our inspiration.

Earlier in this chapter, I purposely told a story about the birth of a child to underscore how wonder can be inspired when we meet our limits. Childbirth, even when supported by modern science, is harrowing. It breaks us up. It makes us "porous." Being with a person at the time of their death can do the same thing. Death rearranges our mental maps. Few today, at least among developed nations, routinely experience life at its limits, up close and personally. Our food comes shrink-wrapped. Or we consume it on the run after a fast food drive-by. Life and death are increasingly abstractions. Awe and mystery are consequently diminished. Reality is desacralized. We

---

5. Polanyi, *The Tacit Dimension*.
6. Polanyi, *Personal Knowledge*.

are "buffered." Perhaps hospice and natal chaplaincy should be required training for all humans. Harrowing is good for the soul. It makes us porous, more fully human, and thus alive to the possibilities of a wonder-driven ministry.

I want to make a case for wonder not at the periphery of ministry but at the center, not simply during extreme moments but moment by moment over a lifetime. I'm betting that if we lived with wonder at the center we'd be far less exhausted and far more energized; far more hopeful and far less cynical; far more resilient and far less brittle. In short, we would be enchanted by awesome mystery. There are two principal challenges to that kind of ministry: acedia and hubris. There are also two antidotes: grace-tempered pride and the gift of humility. Both sponsor leadership marked by resiliency, as I hope to bear testimony to in the chapters that follow.

For Reflection and Discussion

1. We say that God is always present yet it appears that God is "more" present at some times than at others. Since God is always present, what do we mean when we pray for God to be near? Why do we invoke God before we preach or break bread or begin meetings? Is God more present after we pray? Are we more attentive? Some of both?

2. When was the last time you experienced the presence of God? What did you experience? What did you feel? What did you think? What difference did it make afterwards?

3. God's holiness is a large biblical category. When God appears, Moses hides his face, Isaiah is undone, and the disciples disbelieve with joy. Can we presume to know too much about God? If so, what negative impacts might that have on how ministry is conceived or how ministers see themselves?

4. In your work, do you ever worry about being the resident religious expert, the professional? How does being a religious professional impact the way you experience God? Might professionalism become a cause of "buffering"? If so, how might it be countered?

5. The story of the birth of a child was told as an example of a time when life "breaks us up" by bringing us to our limits (in this case, emotional limits—the fear of death, the miracle of birth). When have you been

broken up or "harrowed"? In that time how did you experience wonder, enchantment, or awe over the mystery we know as God?

6. Think about the role wonder plays in discovery. Think about the role intuition plays. The former motivates; the latter tells us where to start searching. Can God use daydreams? Can God use hunches? Why or why not? Do any Scripture texts come to mind as you consider the role of hunches or dreams in God's mysterious role in our lives? What biblical characters had dreams that became significant in their experience of God? How do we "moderns" relate to those experiences?

7. Doctrine is important; study is important; scholarship is important. Most ministers value all three. Do you ever worry about being too reasonable? How are Word and Spirit related; reason and emotion; order and ardor? Must these always be binary or opposed? Do you ever long to know what your ministry would look like if these were more fused, mashed together? How might your ministry be different if they were?

CHAPTER TWO

Acedia and Grace-Tempered Pride

The Cicada's Song

If acedia (literally, not *caring*) had a theme song it would be sung by the cicada, the seventeen-year North American genus alternately known as the *jar fly* or *dog-day cicada*. Why the cicada? Because it spends most of its life in the dark, underground, sucking tree sap through a long proboscis before emerging in late July or August when it molts, leads a brief life singing—up to 120 decibels or twice our normal speaking voice—and then dies.

Cicadas are loud. They hum on and on. Actually, the females don't sing, only the males, which is not to suggest that acedia is gender specific; it is not. The cicada or tree cricket sings to attract a mate. Some species have a lower volume distress call and still others a quiet courtship song signaling successful mating, but that loud humming heard in mid-August when it's 102 degrees and the only thing moving is your dog's tail, swatting flies, is our friend's signature song.

Cicadas have five eyes: two big red ones on the sides of their heads and three smaller ones located in between. Don't let their menacing appearance fool you. Cicadas are mostly harmless unless your arm happens to be mistaken for a tree branch and out comes that nasty proboscis, but that's rare—you're likely to brush one off way before that happens.

Cicadas mostly get inside your head—that humming, sizzling, makes-you-want-to-run-and-hide song of theirs—which to me sounds like a lament, maybe a favorite cheatin' heart country song. Once mating is complete, the cicada is done, the male anyway—females live long enough to drop up to six hundred eggs in as many as fifty nests before they die. Once hatched, the nymphs drop from their tree-branch nests and burrow one to eight feet underground until they find a fat, tasty root to suck on for the next seventeen years. And then they're out again. No wonder they cry so fiercely in the light of day!

The song "Acedia" sung by the cicada is no laughing matter. Acedia gets inside you like the persistent humming of the cicada that sort of drills away at you. While classically known as sloth or laziness, I think *not caring* comes closer to its meaning. When I think about acedia and what it does to us, verses six and seven of Psalm 30 come to mind:

> As for me, I said in my prosperity,
> "I shall never be moved."
> By your favor, O Lord,
> you had established me as a strong mountain;
> you hid your face;
> I was dismayed.

Acedia is like what we feel when a trusted friend won't look at us. Maybe we did something to harm the relationship and maybe we didn't, but our friend, whom we see, is not looking at us. We feel shunned, alone, disconnected, which can give rise to listlessness, laziness, detachment. Acedia is a state or condition. I am persuaded that it's not uncommon among ministers. While it has depression-like characteristics, acedia is a spiritual malady. It robs us of imagination and wonder and consequently striving or drive. I hope to show that our greatest weapon against it is not bravado, but the gift of grace-tempered pride, a graced vulnerability that allows us to end secrecy, silence, and exile when we reconnect with the communion of saints and the living One who calls us *friends*.

At its heart, acedia turns us inward, trapping us in what Barth defined as the closed circle of our humanity.[1] Acedia robs us of wonder. Tempered pride, the willingness to accept our humanity and rejoin the human race, gives us power to bounce back for the work God calls us to do. Tempered pride, owning our God-given humanity, restores wonder grounded in the One who "is the image of the invisible God" (Col 1:15), the Word made flesh, Jesus Christ.

In order to better understand acedia, I want to tell a story that's very close to me and then one shared with the permission of my friend, John

---

1. Barth, *The Epistle to the Romans*, 253.

Mulder. John's story in his own words appears in the May 2010 issue of *Perspectives,* titled "Pilgrim's Progress: You Can't Make It Alone." The first story I tell is my own.

Keep Walking

Five months after my twenty-eighth birthday and eight months after the birth of my second child, my fifty-six-year-old father had a heart attack and died. Three months later, my wife and I packed our bags and two young children, and moved east to our home state where I accepted my second call. Eighteen months later, I began Doctor of Ministry studies. Life was busy, but mostly good. I was enthused by my new job, happy at home, and challenged by my academic pursuit. I was "prospering," or thought I was. In retrospect, I buried my grief with my father. I didn't allow myself time or space to grieve. I didn't express my grief. And I was poised to bury even more.

The church I served needed new parking, a mundane goal, but nonetheless desired. We had plenty of space—thirteen acres—and a little bit of money, not a lot but enough to pave the gravel lot then in use. In order to authorize spending what amounted to roughly one-tenth of the annual budget for the improvement, a congregational meeting was called. A letter from the church board endorsing the project was mailed out along with a plan for funding it. With the money in hand and the board in agreement, I expected a routine congregational vote and no opposition.

The meeting was conducted following a Sunday service. In my tradition, the pastor is not a member of the congregation, but moderates its meetings. After worship, I called the meeting to order, offered prayer, and asked for the property and finance committees to report. With the reports complete and a motion made, the floor was open for discussion.

Tim, an elder in my church, was seated near the front. After one or two others spoke, Tim raised his hand. While Tim was not an active elder at the time, he was a past board member and regular worship attendee. Tim had also served on the search committee that led to my call. I considered him a friend. When Tim stood to speak, he turned his back to me and faced the congregation. From his tone and his words, Tim was clearly opposed to paving the parking lot.

This was maybe the third or fourth congregational meeting I had ever moderated and the first ever where I felt responsible for the outcome. I was nervous. I was also about to be really stupid. I wanted that parking lot. I thought we needed it. In the heat of the moment and with my heart pounding, I interrupted Tim and said to him in my best preacher voice, "Tim, address the moderator."

I had witnessed that procedure at presbytery meetings: "Address the moderator." I had also read the prescribed protocol in *Robert's Rules of Order*. At the time I chose to use the move, it seemed like a good idea, a way of keeping order. But, if truth be told, it was a way of getting what I wanted. Alas, instead of order, the wheels came off.

Tim was hard of hearing. His wife would say, "Deaf as a post." When I called out to him in front of the ninety souls gathered for the meeting, he was puzzled, addled, thrown off his game. He looked at me like, "What are you saying?" and then turned his back again and continued speaking. I felt threatened: how dare he turn his back on the moderator. My heart raced. He was addressing the congregation and not me. They were *his* people and not *mine*. I felt like I was being ruled out. So, I said to him again, "Tim, address the moderator."

This time I not only befuddled Tim, but also embarrassed him. He lost his train of thought. Red-faced, he sat down. As soon as my clever words were out of my mouth, I knew I had done the wrong thing. I felt like an ass. I don't remember what was said next, just that the vote was taken and passed. I got my parking lot. Whoopie! But in doing so, I had embarrassed a friend and disgraced myself.

Thirty years ago I didn't know anything about panic attacks, but I was having one even if I couldn't name it. I felt horrible. A lump crawled in my throat and took up residence. I was frightened, ashamed, embarrassed. That afternoon I called Tim and asked if I could come by that evening. He agreed. I went to his house and apologized. I was truly sorry. He accepted my apology, sort of, but told me he thought it would be "awhile" before he would be back in church. I left feeling worse than when I went. But that wasn't all. Word came to me that Tim's friend's best friend, Barry, was mad at me. Barry, a board member, had not attended the congregational meeting but had heard through the grapevine about my actions. Barry, known to have an ill, short temper, let it be known to any who would listen that he was having nothing to do with *moderator* George Sinclair.

One month went by. Tim and Barry made good on their promises. They boycotted worship and everyone knew why. And, if Barry hadn't made the "why" clear indirectly he was about to do so explicitly.

A day-long, out-of-town, officer retreat had been set some weeks before the ill-fated congregational meeting. Twelve served on the board. On the day of the retreat only eleven showed up—Barry was missing.

Prior to the retreat and knowing that he was angry at me, I had tried through a third party to meet with Barry. He had refused. Barry was a neighbor, literally. I could see his house from my house. He had also been on the pastoral search committee through which I was called to the congregation. I liked him. He was an assistant coach for a local high school football team. Since I had played football as a kid, we hit it off. No matter, he not only refused to see me, he let the board know why.

Just after breakfast and morning worship at our retreat, and just before starting our day-long planning, Will, a fellow elder, asked if he could read a letter. When Will raised his hand I had a suspicion it might not be good news. And it wasn't. Barry was resigning and I was the problem. Barry stated in his letter that he was quitting in view of "recent actions" taken by the *moderator*. Will later told me that Barry wanted it to be a "bombshell." And it was. The lump that had never completely left my chest returned with a vengeance. I don't know how I made it through the retreat, but I managed. It was hell.

On the trip home, I wanted to scream. It felt like the walls of the van were closing in. I had to escape. I wanted to get away from *these* people, *this* church, which no longer felt like my church. I felt alone. I felt cut off. I tried telling myself that "I didn't care," but deep down I did care and it was killing me.

I did manage to make it home that day and not to jump out of the van, but misery was another thing. I couldn't shake it. I obsessed about what had happened. I replayed my actions a thousand times. And every time, the tape ended at the exact same place.

They say time heals all wounds. Not this one. It would not go away. It wasn't like church was going badly. The ripple of the meeting died down soon enough, but not the storm inside of me. My studies continued without incident; I marshaled on, but I wasn't the same. Fall led to winter and winter to spring. I preached every week, taught, tried to be a good husband and father, but I was miserable. I couldn't get that day or the feelings associated with it out of my heart. I felt desperately alone. I burrowed underground like our friend the cicada, unable to see the light. I was present but detached, surrounded by people, but alone. Acedia.

With summer approaching and my Doctor of Ministry work nearing completion, my wife and I planned a family vacation, a trip to the beach. Just what I needed, or so I thought.

The beach weather was picture perfect. We spent a great first day; the kids had a blast. That night I drank, a lot. "Numb out. That's the ticket." The next morning, I felt like crap. In a fit of remorse, I gathered what was left of the booze and poured it out. "Maybe that will make me feel better." It did, sort of, but I checked, and sure enough, the old familiar lump was still in my chest, like a clump of butterflies flapping their wings.

Since I was up before the sun and my family, I went down to the beach for a walk by myself. "That's the spirit. Surely God will meet me on the beach?" I felt nothing. There was a beautiful sunrise, but I couldn't feel God. I believed in God. I believed in the abstraction called "God." And I prayed. I prayed continuously, but I couldn't feel God. And "feel" isn't an adequate word. I suffered from spiritual malady. I couldn't love God or know God's love. God was a distant idea.

I don't know how far I walked that morning. I don't know what I expected or hoped to encounter. I was just walking, wandering. The sun was still low on the horizon but bright enough for my eye to catch motion down the beach, up next to the dunes. With nothing better to do, I went for a look. It was a sea turtle. It must have been three feet across the back. She was laying eggs, using her hind flippers to cover them with sand. I'd never seen anything like it. I sat down and watched. With the last egg covered, she headed back to the sea.

It must have been thirty, maybe forty yards to the breakwater. The sea turtle would take two or three steps and plop down, two or three more and plop down again. This went on for thirty minutes or so. I'm watching her, keeping my distance, but moving with her as she moves toward the water. She's got an eye on me, but mostly her head is down and she's heading for the sea.

When she makes it to ankle deep water, the going gets easier; when she makes it to the wash, easier still. Finally, in waist deep water, she takes off. And I get this vibe from her like, "Look at me!" And then she was gone. As soon as she hit waist deep water, that was it. She was gone, safe, at home.

I'm thinking to myself, "Lord, is this the best you've got? Moses got a burning bush and I get a sea turtle?" I wish I could tell you that my spirit lifted and I broke out in song, but that didn't happen, not right away, anyway. I left the beach that morning with one thought: life is hard. Life is a struggle. That's what I got. That's what the sea turtle taught me—life is difficult; it's a struggle. You're going to get tired and plop down, but even when it's hard there is hope. Keep walking.

There's a wonderful quote attributed to St. Augustine. My friend John Mulder told me he taped it to his desk: *Solvitur ambulando*—"It is solved by walking." That's what the turtle taught me: keep walking, even when it's hard, even when the way forward is not clear or easy, keep walking.

I did eventually get better. I can't locate a point in time, but the lump in my throat finally bid me farewell. I know one thing: I could never have made it without my wife's constant listening and encouragement and the support I received from my friend Randy, a Methodist preacher and golfing buddy. If I had to date the day wonder returned, it would be the day I phoned the ball coach. I reached a place where I had finally had enough, enough of myself always being afraid and enough of not doing more about it. So, I picked up the phone, "Barry, can I see you?" He answered, "Yes."

I walked the hundred yards to his house. I had rehearsed what I would say a million times, but that all left when Barry opened the door. He smiled and asked me in.

The coach was an angry man, but a man of sorrows too. He had lost a child five or so years before our arrival, a nine-year-old. She had been playing on the church merry-go-round, her head tossed back the way children do, when the blood vessel ruptured. People have sorrows. People have anger.

When I knocked on the door, coach waved me in. The next thirty minutes blew me away. I said I was sorry. He said he was sorry. There were no angry words, no shouting, only kindness. Barry said, "I guess, George, what I'm trying to say to you is . . . will you be my pastor again?" Barry didn't have to finish. We embraced. In that moment, pride, my pride and Barry's, was tempered by grace. He and I both made it to the sea.

The Hidden God

Acedia is a heart problem, a wonder problem. Acedia robs us of the ability to imagine. It isolates us. It sends us underground, into hiding. When acedia attacks, we perceive that we are alone, cut off from communion. Acedia may manifest as boredom or laziness or nonchalance, addictions even, but fundamentally, acedia is a malady of the heart disconnected from the Source of Life. But I think there is more.

"You hid your face; I was dismayed" (Ps 30: 7).

The Psalmist connected fortune and misfortune with God's face. When things were going well, God was all smiles. When they went badly, God turned away. We wonder why God would do that? Isn't God supposed to be with us—always—to love us and care for us? Aren't the hairs of our head numbered? Doesn't God provide daily bread? Why then do we experience God's absence? Does God hide his face like a friend who refuses to look at you?

Sometimes it feels that way. Is that all on us? If we only got it right, prayed just right, loved just right, had faith, would there be an experience of the hidden God? I don't think so. God is not obvious, even in the best of times God is not obvious. Think about the ten lepers of Luke 17:11–19. Ten were healed but only one returned. What about the nine? Did the nine not experience God's favor? Had not God smiled on them? Why didn't they connect?

Connecting with God is not easy even when God's favor is obvious, even when we prosper and enjoy blessing. How much more difficult is it when things do not go well? "You hid your face; I was dismayed."

We do not manage the hidden God. God is not a jack-in-the-box, crank the handle just so and out he pops. But God does show up. God does appear, not always as we expect and many times as we least expect. But God shows up. Acedia is a particularly dangerous sin because the more we try to force God's appearance, the less God seems to comply. That's been my experience, anyway, and I don't think I'm alone.

Presence

In October 2003, John Mulder, then president of Louisville Presbyterian Theological Seminary, went to Atlanta for treatment for alcoholism. News of his alcoholism and the moral wreckage of his life raced not only through the grapevine but also through national and church media. John had raised millions for Louisville Seminary and was instrumental in the choice of Louisville as the site for the PCUSA's national headquarters. He was also widely known for his academic work. Now he was known for something else.

When John left Louisville for Atlanta he was clinically depressed and overwhelmed by shame and guilt. Only his wife and children pulled him back from the despair of suicide.

John prayed every day. His prayer was always the same: that God and those he had hurt would forgive him. Entering treatment he was told that he had "toxic levels of shame and guilt."[2] In the words of one counselor, he was "spiritually bankrupt."[3] Yet John continued to pray, praying for forgiveness, praying that the deep wounds he had caused would be healed. And he got nothing, absolutely nothing. "You hid your face and I was dismayed."

Discouraged and despairing, John says he "gave up" and reduced his prayer to one request: "Lord, open me up." For more than a month, that was John's prayer: "Lord, open me up." One day, God answered. John wasn't in chapel. He wasn't watching a sunset. He wasn't reading his Bible or praying or singing; he was spreading peanut butter on an English muffin for breakfast in the apartment he shared with three other men. The day was December 9, 2003, two months into treatment. This is how John describes what happened: "Gradually but with intensity, I was aware of a bright, white light around me. It did not last long. I heard no voices or words except one in my head as the light receded: 'You are not alone.'"[4] That was it. And that was enough, or, not quite.

Reflecting on his experience, John observes that "awareness of God's *presence* preceded any sense . . . of God's *forgiveness*."[5] Forgiveness would take more time. Forgiveness came more gradually, slowly, and took people. It took reconnecting with those he had hurt. It took asking for help. John was able to ask for that help because he recognized that he was not alone. He was not alone in his humanity before the hidden God who does not remain hidden. When God shows up we are reconnected with our own humanity and with others.

Acedia is healed by the courage to acknowledge our need for other human beings. We are not alone. We walk with others. We never escape the "closed circle of our humanity," but we do find healing when we walk with others. "To see your face," Jacob told Esau, "is like seeing the face of God" (Gen 33:10).

To see the face of God, we must not only let others see us, we must "see" them.

Some years after his recovery, John Mulder grew curious about relapse. Once escaped, the hell of alcoholism should be enough to keep

2. Mulder, "Pilgrim's Progress," 8.
3. Ibid.
4. Ibid., 8–9
5. Ibid., 9

anyone from going back, but it doesn't—people relapse, they return. They don't stay the course. One often cited reason, John observes, is that relapsers don't work the program—they don't go to meetings; they don't talk to their sponsors; they don't meditate or pray. Others suggest that relapsers ignore or forget the character defects and behaviors that got them into trouble in the first place. In John's view, "relapsers relapse by relying upon themselves, believing that they are 'bullet proof' (the term most often used), believing that they can make it on their own."[6]

When it comes to acedia, we are our own worst enemies. And we are our worst enemy when we fail to get outside of ourselves. Like the cicada, we burrow underground. We think we're safe when we are hiding, when we are buried deep where no one can see us, where no one knows our flaws, our secrets, our shame, our fears, in short, our humanity. But there's hope.

The hidden God calls. "The voice over the waters speaks," sometimes in a *low murmur* or if you prefer in "a sound of sheer silence" (1 Kgs 19:12) or in the "still small voice" of Elijah fame or in sea turtles or unexplained light.

Elijah and the Cicada

In a March 2012 TED Talk, Brené Brown suggests that shame is "highly correlated with addiction, depression, violence, bullying, suicide, eating disorders."[7] I wonder if Elijah was a bully. I'm convinced he was depressed. After his fire contest and Jezebel's threat, Elijah "fled for his life." When he arrived at Beer-sheba, which was the last watering hole before the wilderness, he left his servant and went on *alone*, found a "solitary broom tree" and "asked that he might die." Maybe Elijah was dealing with shame? Clearly he was dealing with acedia. He had stopped caring. God had other plans. God fed him not once or twice but enough to walk forty days to Horeb and the very cave where Moses once hid. And yes, God was about to pass by, just like in the old days.

Before Elijah turned in for the night, the word of the Lord came to him, not so much a statement or declaration but a question: "What are you doing here, Elijah" (1 Kgs 19:9)?

Elijah gave his best shot, his most pious prophetic answer: "I have been very zealous for the LORD, the God of hosts; for the Israelites have

6. Ibid.
7. Brown, "Listening to Shame."

forsaken your covenant, thrown down your altars, and killed your prophets with the sword. I alone am left, and they are seeking my life, to take it away" (1 Kgs 19:10).

Poor Elijah, nobody else but him; he's it. Ain't nobody got it as bad as him. Ain't nobody like him. He's all alone. Or not quite. God is about to pass by. And does God ever pass by—there comes a wind so strong the mountains split, rocks break in pieces, and after the wind, a terrible earthquake comes, and after the earthquake a mighty fire.

Now, you'd think Elijah would be used to these kinds of displays. Elijah's career began with a blast just like that. But God was not in the fire or the earthquake or the wind. When the storm ended there was just a sound. Translators aren't agreed. They can't settle on one translation. The most famous (and I think poorest) is the "still small voice." People like that one because they think the story is about "conscience" or "the voice of reason" or something akin to that—nothing raucous or awe inspiring, nothing that would get in the way of a reasonable faith.

The same Hebrew phrase appears in Psalm 107:29: "he made the storm be still, and the waves over the sea were hushed," which brings to mind "the calm after a storm," not exactly a noise, but sound of some kind. Personally, I prefer "low murmuring" for a translation. Elijah hears the murmuring and checks it out. The murmuring gets him off his duff and out of the cave or at least to its entrance, where he stands and wraps his face in his mantle. Elijah heard something. I'm betting it was cicadas! They come out after thunder clouds break. They go crazy after a hard rain. Misery is a sound!

Here's the thing, Elijah is no different for hearing the "still small voice" or "sound of sheer silence" or "low murmuring." He's the same old Elijah. When cross-examined by the Word at the mouth of the cave, he gives the exact same answer that he gave before God passed by: "I have been very zealous . . . I alone am left." But the story doesn't end there. God's not finished. Elijah has a mission. He is sent. "Go to Damascus . . . anoint Hazael as king . . . anoint Juhu . . . and anoint Elisha . . . as prophet *in your place*" (1Kgs 19:16; emphasis mine).

That's a fine "how do you do." And not only that, God concludes their tête-à-tête by letting Elijah in on a little secret: "There are 7,000 others back home and a bunch more like them who are equally zealous for me, so get over yourself, Elijah, and get busy. Rejoin humanity." Tempered pride.

I don't exactly feel sorry for Elijah; I mean I do and I don't. I feel empathy with him. In fact, I probably see more of myself in him than I care to admit. Like most of us, Elijah wants to have his cake and eat it too. But we can't have it both ways. We can't always be big and powerful and never small and weak. Paul talks about God's power being perfected in weakness. Acedia teaches us just how weak we can become—all alone. But we're not alone. That's the good news. There are 7,000 others just like us, 7,000 others who have felt or will feel ashamed or alone or lost in the "closed circle of their humanity."

We never get over our humanity but we can embrace it, and that requires courage inspired by grace. When I made a fool of myself in front of my congregation, I tried every way I could to tell myself that I hadn't acted like a jackass. I learned that I could run and hide from being a jackass but never stopped being one. And that's okay. God works with what he has and what he has is us—flawed human beings.

Face it; we're not always spiritual. We're not always connected. We're not always in touch with the holy. Wonder doesn't work that way. Sometimes that's our fault. But sometimes, sometimes God simply hides. I don't know why that is so, I only know it to be true. God is not always obvious. God is not always felt or experienced or present to us. And I'm not going to put that all on us, as if we only need to act differently or have better faith or hold our mouth right when we pray and God will show his face. It just doesn't work that way.

But I do know this: God is never without a witness. God never stops calling us. It might be a sea turtle on a lonesome beach. It might be a mysterious light convincing us that we are not alone. It might be a low murmuring sound or the sound of misery; okay, a cicada, I said it. However drawn, however found, however contacted, we are drawn by wondrous grace to a human face, to a human touch, and to a Voice that tells us, "You are not alone. I am with you always to the close of the age." And that word is enough.

The antidote to acedia is grace-tempered pride, courage to join the human race one step, one day, one song at a time. *Solvitur ambulando*. "It is solved by walking." It is the grace of wonder, the grace of the "voice over the waters" calling us to get up and get moving.

For Reflection and Discussion

1. Acedia need not be inspired by public foolishness or addiction; it may simply present as boredom. An intern once told me that he had just

gotten off the phone with a friend in his first call as a solo pastor. His friend bragged about it being 11a.m. and he was at his office desk playing a video game and no one was the wiser. May boredom be a sign of acedia? If so, how?

2. When I told my father that I was going into ministry he said he had considered it but felt he could not set the right kind of example. Have you ever labored under that kind of pressure? If so, how has it affected your ministry? What has the need for perfection done to you? Are you ever fearful of being seen as fully and genuinely flawed?

3. What has been your greatest public embarrassment in ministry? How did it affect you and what did you learn from it?

4. Who do you regularly talk to about your ministry and life? Who sees you as you are and what has that meant for your ministry?

5. What do you do to fight acedia?

6. How do you manage to be vulnerable and yet maintain boundaries in your professional life?

7. Have you experienced God's absence? What was it like? How did you bounce back? What or who brought you back?

CHAPTER THREE

Hubris and the Gift of Humility

Star?

May 1968. Junior High School Awards Day. 9:00 a.m.

When I entered the auditorium my eyes lit up. Center stage held a treasure trove of trophies: Most Valuable Football; Most Valuable Basketball; Most Valuable Baseball; Most Valuable Track; Best All Around. When I sat down in the wooden theater seat, a friend poked me in the ribs: "Hey, George, turn around; your parents are here." Sure enough, there they were. My heart skipped—"One of those trophies must be for me."

I knew it wasn't baseball. I couldn't hit a curve. And I knew it wasn't basketball. I was too clumsy. I doubted it was track. They don't give trophies for field events, not for second place. "Maybe it was football?" For two years I had started on both sides of the ball, but trophies went to stars like the quarterback or halfback. I was a lowly lineman. They don't give linemen trophies, at least not in junior high. So what was it? Surely my parents hadn't come unless I was being recognized. It wasn't going to be for perfect attendance or the math or science award. They don't award *Average*. And when it came to grades I was average.

By 9:45 the principal had given the perfect attendance awards and the math and science awards and had recognized the band students and the chorus and the cheerleaders and the guys in the AV Room. Now it was time for the stars—the big guns—the players, the athletes. The principal yielded the podium to the coaches.

The track award went to Robert; basketball to Rob; baseball to Tim; football to Wayne; Best All Around to Wade. There was one trophy left. "This year's award for Most Improved Athlete goes to George Sinclair." My heart pounded. When I reached center stage I couldn't feel my legs. And from the smile on my fourteen-year-old face when they took our picture thirty minutes later I sure looked happy—me in my double-breasted blue blazer, brass buttons, white turtleneck. Hey, it was 1968!

May 1986. Seminary Commencement. 7:00 p.m.

While working on my Doctor of Ministry, I worked full-time as the pastor of a 150-member church. The time had come to march and receive my diploma. My wife, children, and mother made the trip across two states, along with an aunt and uncle, who stood in for my deceased father. It was a big night. It had been a long haul. My Doctor of Ministry project, a commentary and study guide on the Apostles' Creed, ran over two hundred pages. I had enjoyed the work, but was glad to have it finished.

Eight years earlier in the same seminary chapel, while waiting to receive my Masters, I read through the names of classmates I had spent three years with and noted a much shorter list of doctoral students. One or two of the doctoral students had an asterisk beside their name. The footnote to the tiny star read, *With Distinction*. I tucked the star away and forgot about it, or almost. I waited eight years to remember it. As we robed up to process into the chapel, the thought crossed my mind, "I wonder if I'm going to graduate *With Distinction*? I put in a lot of hours. That stuff I wrote about epistemology was good. What can it hurt, just a tiny star. That's all I ask."

Alas, when I received a program and saw my name, there was no asterisk, no star, just my name. "Well, maybe they don't award that anymore," I told myself. "What does it matter? It was just a silly star." But it did matter. In a secret part of me, it smarted.

March 2013. AKC Championships. Pensacola, Florida. 11:00 a.m.

On this date, Blue Note's Brilliant Corners, an Australian Shepherd, more commonly known as "Monk," and sired by Starswepts HiFlying of Warner Robbins, Georgia, won his first American Kennel Club Championship. The three-year-old Aussie had shown at Spartanburg, Hendersonville, Greenville, Atlanta, Perry, Gulfport, Hattiesburg, Roanoke, and other southeastern cities. It is unknown whether Monk's mother, Lyric's Follow Me, also of Warner Robbins, responded favorably to Monk's achievement. Meanwhile, the shepherd's breeder was ecstatic as was Monk's handler, who told reporters, "I always knew that Monk was a Champion."

Monk's current owners told me that Monk was indifferent to his Pensacola success. They said he could have cared less about the championship. He was the same old Monk, though they did note traces of envy displayed by Monk's cousin Charlie of Washington, DC—a commoner of no title!

A Particular Kind of Pride

So what is it about us? Why do we care about stars and awards, degrees and pedigrees? Can we not work for work's sake? Can we not study for study's sake? Must even play turn into competition? Why can't humans be more like Monk? Of course, in a pack, even dogs will fight for first place. Are canines and humans predisposed to pride or that more ancient sin labeled hubris?

H. Richard Niebuhr argues that Jesus did not confuse humility with self-abnegation, or feelings of inferiority or the old realm's notion of "keeping one's place."[1] Rather, Jesus "spoke with authority and acted with confidence. . . . His humility," Niebuhr observes, "is of the sort that raises to a new sense of dignity and worth those who have been humiliated. . . . It is a kind of proud humility and humble pride."[2] Said otherwise, grace lifts us up. Grace tempers pride.

Two ideas are central to tempered pride. The first is expressed in Genesis: we are dust. The second is in Psalm 8: we are a little lower than God. Tempered hubris, like tempered acedia, is birthed and nurtured when we hold with wonder our time and place in God's creation, and when we yield to the mystery of gospel treasure carried in the clay jars we are. Before exploring the inspiration of tempered pride, I want to pause and first consider some examples that illustrate how hubris or excessive pride slips into parish life. The stories and names are fictional, the characters real.

---

1. Niebuhr, *Christ and Culture*, 26–27.
2. Ibid.

Greg's Borkum Riff

Greg developed an affinity for burley tobacco in high school. By college it had become in his mind an attractive addiction. He relished mornings spent in the campus library discussing Tillich with his favorite professor and never once thought that a twenty-year-old looked foolish with a pipe stuck in his mouth. By the time he donned his Geneva gown and accepted his first call to ministry, the pipe was a constant companion.

Greg's church office measured eight by twelve feet. A mad architect with a penchant for doors must have designed it, or more likely, the office was an afterthought—a good place for the preacher to read, write, or pop into the pulpit through door number one, or into the nave through door number two, or to escape outdoors through door number three. Greg had only recently fired up a fresh bowl of Borkum Riff when there was a knock at door number two. With pipe in hand, Greg got up from his desk, took four short steps to door number two and opened it. "Ah, good morning, Bertha, won't you come in."

Bertha was not happy. Bertha was never happy. And she was really unhappy when she waded into Greg's Swedish tobacco-filled office. "Why I never," Bertha began. "I can't believe you, our preacher, would smoke, much less smoke in your office. You can smell the smoke all the way out in the sanctuary."

"Must smell good out there," Greg thought to himself, but he kept his mouth shut. "Why, I never," Bertha scowled. "You ought to be ashamed." And with that she turned on her heel and left through door number two.

Greg relit his pipe and sat down dumbfounded. "In seminary, everybody smoked. The old biddy, who does she think she is coming in *my* office and telling *me* how to live *my* life? Nobody's going to tell me what to do. This is *my* space. Old busybody, I'll show her."

What should Greg do? Keep smoking and tell Bertha to take a hike? Ignore Bertha and smoke outside on the front porch of the church? Quit smoking?

Elise's Cause

Elise was passionate about advocacy for gay and lesbian causes. Her denomination was sharply divided over the ordination issue. Elise knew where she stood and wasn't shy about telling others. Her prayers and sermons reflected her open and inclusive stance.

Bill, a forty-two-year-old church elder and father of two school-age boys, had other ideas. He was frustrated with Elise. He couldn't understand why her prayers always had to mention "the gay thing." Finally, after one sermon and one prayer too many, he had had enough. On Monday, he called Elise and asked for an appointment. Elise agreed. They met for coffee.

"I just don't understand," Bill began. "I don't see why you won't leave the gay issue alone. Can't you tone it down? It seems like every other sermon has to have some illustration about how badly gays are treated. And if it's not your sermons, it's your prayers. Why can't you tone it down? There are two sides to every issue and I feel like our church is only hearing one."

What should Elise do? Give Bill equal time in the pulpit? Challenge him to a public debate? Invite Bill to co-teach a Sunday school class with her on "Homosexuality and the Bible"? What?

Henry's Salary

Henry's salary was up for review, an annual requirement of his denomination. Henry hated the process and hated the idea that everybody in the church knew his personal finances. But it was a necessity, or so Henry convinced himself. At least nobody could accuse him of getting rich, which, given the small church Henry served, was unlikely.

The salary review process was straightforward—the personnel committee spent thirty minutes with Henry asking a few general questions about his work. Then the personnel committee reported to the church board, which set a raise or not based on pledge receipts for the coming year. Money was always tight in Henry's small-town church. Even in good years, he never expected more than a two or three percent raise, if that. Henry did good work and enjoyed support from his church board. They recommended a three percent increase, which, given his already small salary, only added a few hundred dollars more each month. But it was a help.

Henry's salary was voted on each January. The meetings were held after worship in the church fellowship hall—casseroles, congealed salads, and ham for the main course followed by ample servings of homemade pies and assorted deserts. It wasn't the food that gave Henry indigestion, just the thought of the vote. By custom, once the meeting was called to order and terms presented, Henry turned over the gavel to the congregation's secretary and excused himself so that members could "speak their mind." Henry left and waited to be retrieved after the vote was taken.

Most votes were uncontested, with maybe a comment or two about how soybean prices were down and how that would impact the budget, but most years were uneventful and Henry was back at the moderator's stand in ten minutes tops. This year was different. This year Terrence stood up and asked for the floor.

Terrence was just a few years older than Henry. He had a wife and three kids, a marginal small farm and a bucket of anger. He dumped a full load at that day's meeting. "Why should Henry get a raise when the rest of us are barely making it? It's just not right. I say we vote No. Preachers shouldn't be in it for the money anyway. Again, my vote is No."

Members had come to expect this sort of thing from Terrence. They listened politely, took the vote and with one or two no votes passed Henry's raise.

Henry could tell by the expression on the messenger's face when he was retrieved that something foul was in the air. "What's up?" Henry plied the messenger with a nervous smile.

"Oh, nothing, you know Terrence, up to his old self—said you shouldn't get a raise and all. But don't worry, it passed. You're in for another year." Henry's blood boiled, "The nerve of that guy? Why does he have to make my life miserable? What did I ever do to him?"

What should Henry do? Forget about Terrence and let him stew? Confront Terrence and find out why he thinks the pastor doesn't deserve a raise? Tell his church board he's tired of Terrence taking pot shots and ask the board to take disciplinary action? Or, just accept the fact that there are people like Terrence in every church?

Sarah's Accused Son

Sarah loved her work as an associate for youth and education. Having her own fifteen-year-old daughter and twelve-year-old son in her program could be tricky but was mostly manageable.

Sarah's church ran a large set of Wednesday night ministries—supper, choir rehearsals, adult studies, children and youth activities—in short, lots of traffic, high energy, and opportunities for mischief. As a veteran youth worker, Sarah had few illusions and a thick skin, or so she thought until a choir member stopped her in a hallway one Wednesday night to let her know that he had heard that Sarah's son, Stephen, had "pushed" his way onto the elevator, injuring a younger child. Sarah felt her face turning red. She didn't believe her son would do such a thing, but it was her job to find out what happened.

After checking with several adults and after talking to her son and the little girl supposedly injured, Sarah concluded that the choir member had heard wrong. Stephen was nowhere around when the child was pushed. Sarah was satisfied that was the end of the matter. In fact, she spoke with the girl's parents to make sure she was all right and her parents explained that their daughter didn't know who knocked her down. There were a lot of older kids running on and off of the elevator and she just didn't know.

Ten days after the episode Sarah's board had a scheduled monthly meeting. Prior to the meeting Sarah read through the agenda and seeing nothing but routine business planned accordingly for an hour-and-a-half meeting. Sarah was in for a surprise. Thirty minutes into the meeting an officer raised his hand and was recognized by the senior pastor conducting the meeting. Wilson, never one to mince words, was something of a whiner, a complainer. "I hear that that boy of Sarah's knocked down little Sally and then bragged about it to his buddies. What are we going to do about it?"

Sarah didn't wait for her boss to ask her to respond. She said, "You weren't there, Wilson. How can you make such a conclusive, snap judgment about my child? You can say anything you want about me and say it to my face, but I'm not going to sit here and take this from you. I'll not stand for it. I've spoken with Sally and her parents. They don't blame Stephen. Where do you get off making unfounded accusations against my child?"

The room grew deathly quiet. The senior pastor cleared his throat. Twenty-three officers either looked down at the floor or squirmed uncomfortably in their jury-styled chairs. Wilson looked withered and crossed his arms as if to say through pinched lips, "I give."

What should Sarah do? Absolutely nothing? Wait for Wilson to apologize? Wait three days and if Wilson doesn't call, call him and offer to sit down and work things out? Or, something else? You be the judge.

Adam's Dream Call

When Adam and Stephanie boarded the plane for the flight home they were on top of the world. It was a dream come true. The church Adam had just interviewed with was a perfect fit—back in their home state, coastal, large, urban, and a last move where Adam could finish his career. Stephanie would have no trouble landing a job in the mid-sized city. It had been a great two-day visit with the search committee. Their last lunch together felt like a welcoming party and when the chair, Marla, drove them around town and to her home they thought the deal was sealed. "We're moving," they thought. The three-year search was coming to a happy end.

Two days passed. No word from the chair. Three days. "I've got a bad feeling," Adam said, shaking his head. "Something's not right. Something has happened. They should have called by now. You don't say, 'When you're our pastor we're going to . . .' and not call unless something has changed. I'm calling Marla."

"Why don't you wait," Stephanie advised. "Give it one more day." Adam agreed.

The next day went by like molasses. Still no call. "Well, I'm not waiting any longer," Adam sighed at four. "I'm calling."

"Hey, Marla, how are things? Stephanie and I hadn't heard from you and thought we'd give you a call to see if you had reached a decision."

Marla stammered, sounding uncomfortable, like it was their first conversation. "Adam, we've decided to go in another direction. I was going to call you later today. It took our committee longer to decide than I had expected. I'm sorry for the delay and I'm sorry things didn't work out."

"That's okay, thanks, Marla. I understand. I wish you the best. I enjoyed meeting you and the other committee members. Give them my regards."

Stephanie felt terrible. The man she had loved for twenty-eight years looked like someone had just kicked him in the stomach. "Can you believe that?" Adam said when he hung up the phone. "I knew something was wrong. Maybe I shouldn't have made that off-hand remark about contemporary music—they're very traditional and Marla made it clear that she loved classical music and sang in the choir. Maybe it's just as well. Maybe I wasn't supposed to go there anyway. It sure felt right. I can't believe it. I can't believe they said all of those nice things about us and acted the way they did over lunch about us coming there. If that's the kind of people they are I don't want to be there anyway."

Adam was angry, disappointed, and racked with self-doubt. When he later learned that the church called a minister half his age it only made matters worse. "Maybe I'm just not that good," Adam thought to himself. "Maybe I'm too old. Maybe my ideas are worn out. Maybe I'm just not that talented or I'm less of a leader than I imagined."

What should Adam do? Lick his wounds? Take a vacation and rethink his aim? Rewrite his resume? Lower his ambition? What?

Pride Redeemed

What kind of pride makes us hypersensitive, resentful, indecisive, over-scrupulous, self-critical, envious? And what kind of pride keeps us human? Was Greg just being stubborn by refusing Bertha's smoking ban? Was Elise being self-righteous? Was Henry right to stand up for his pay raise and Sarah for her wrongly accused child? Was Adam wrong to swing for the stars? "Bad" pride could raise its head in any of these or like situations as could pride tempered by humility. Nothing is set in stone. And that's the point. Sin is always "lurking" at the door (Gen 4:7).

Untempered pride is such an easy trap for ministers: we are put on moral pedestals when we handle the holy, when we baptize and bless, when we pray for the sick, or before our congregations break bread. We are deferred to when we teach or lead group discussions. People treat us differently—we are seldom "just" another person. The question is, "What do we do about it?"

I want to suggest two things: first, that we hold with wonder our time and place in God's creation; and, second, that we yield to the mystery of gospel treasure carried in the clay jars we are. When we do these things, hubris is tempered by grace-inspired humility. We become humble not impotent, responsible not arrogant. Pride that makes us humble thrives when we remember we are dust and live with awe before the beauty and profound mystery of God's grace in Jesus Christ. Pride that makes us "humbly proud" grows in wonder.

Clay Jars

Following Hurricane Katrina, remnants of an ancient cypress forest were discovered in sixty feet of water ten miles off the coast of Fort Morgan, Alabama. Divers exploring the secret location reported swimming along three hundred yards of what appeared to be a river channel snaking through the forest. Scientists first believed the forest dated from between 8,000 and 13,000 years ago. More recent studies suggest that the forest may be 100,000 years old.[3]

I live an hour's drive from Fort Morgan. As the crow flies, it's about thirty miles from my house. I enjoy surf fishing there. The fishing is good and the human population minimal. When I heard about the forest, it blew my mind. How could that be—cypress trees, some stumps five feet across, giants, like redwoods; how could the Mobile-Tensaw Delta have extended that far into the Gulf? Time, that's how, time and a living planet, a 4.5-billion-year-old planet.

"Teach us to count our days that we may gain a wise heart" (Ps 90:12).

Four-point-five billion years is a lot of counting. How to fathom it? Imagine a forty-volume earth history. Each volume in our history contains 1,000 pages, each page holds 1,000 words, and each word represents 100 years. Every page turned equals 100,000 years; every volume 100 million years. Using this scale, the ancient cypress swamp buried under sixty feet of sea water ten miles out in the Gulf of Mexico dates from the very last page of our forty-five volume earth history, which in earth time is no time.

Of course a lot has happened over the last 100,000 years. Seventy-five thousand years ago humans almost disappeared. All but several thousand *homo sapiens* died after a super volcanic eruption in Sumatra, which is one reason why seven billion souls today share such an incredibly small gene pool. But we got busy and as the population grew we spread out, reaching the Americas perhaps 18,000 years ago. Seven thousand years later we started farming. Farming led to cities and cities to writing and writing ultimately to moveable type, which using our earth history calculator was a mere 5.4 words ago! And from then to this present moment, less than the time it takes to read this sentence? Well, maybe the blink of a eye or one-third of a second, which is pretty darn fast, like the passing of our days, which, as the Bible says, "are swifter than a weaver's shuttle" (Job 7:6).

"Teach us to count our days . . ."

Counting days requires truth telling. And we all need help with truth telling. We need someone to hear our truth and speak truth back to us. Hubris dislikes truth. Hubris blurs truth and sometimes ignores truth or erases it altogether.

When Dietrich Bonhoeffer organized his Finkenwalde Seminary, confession was required. Ministers will do well to find someone to hear their confession. No less than others, ministers fall prey to the allure of

---

3. Raines, "Ancient Underwater Forest."

power, competency, significance, virtue, recognition, and other friends of hubris. Pride requires collusion, co-conspirators who collaborate with and reinforce pride's demands. So break the conspiracy, crack open the silence. Find someone who can help you count your days, someone who will help you keep perspective, someone who can help you gain a heart of wisdom.

God doesn't expect perfection. God expects us to confess our sins to one another. We need someone who will hear our truth and who will tell us the truth. We all need someone who will help us "count our days," someone who helps us remember that we are dust and to dust we return.

Dust doesn't make us dirt. Dust doesn't make us worthless. Dust reminds us that in the scheme of God's time we're not all that important, not our failures or our accomplishments.

"Vanity of vanities," says the Preacher. "All is vanity" (Eccl 1:2). We're just not that important. Recognizing vanity doesn't lead to nihilism; it leads to freedom. It leads to freedom from placing too much importance on our importance—the hospital call we didn't make; the budget that was not fully pledged; the sermon preached that brought not a word of response, recognition, or appreciation. Remembering we are dust does not diminish our work; it frees us to let go of pride's false promise: "You will be approved when your church is growing. You will be approved when people like your sermons. You will be approved when you are recognized in the city square. You will be approved when . . ."

We are dust, in which God breathes the breath of life. Hold that reality with wonder. It will temper your vanity. But also live knowing that God created us "a little lower than God." We are created, yes, from dust, but created to serve God's creation. We carry gospel treasure in clay jars. Consider Paul and his tumult in Corinth.

Vessels of Hope

Paul had a confidence problem in Corinth. Could the Corinthians trust him and the gospel he preached? The confidence problem cut two ways—the Corinthians doubted Paul and Paul doubted himself. The confidence problem at Corinth swirled around credibility. Why should the Corinthians take Paul at his word? Why should they believe him, trust his leadership, accept his guidance?

Paul's relationship with the Corinthian church started out with trust, but a short time after he left them, things soured: perhaps because those

Paul names "super-apostles" sewed seeds of doubt; perhaps because instead of visiting face-to-face Paul wrote a "harsh, frank" letter dealing with sexual misconduct leaving an open wound in the community; perhaps because while Paul taught that grace was free he asked for money for the saints in Jerusalem; perhaps because wealthy patrons were insulted because Paul refused to let them pay his salary; perhaps because the same large donors were still smarting from the tongue lashing Paul gave them for excluding poor members from the Lord's table; perhaps because Paul scolded the Corinthians for taking each other to court; perhaps because the Corinthians were put off by Paul's hubris—"Pharisee of Pharisees" only now "Christian of Christians;" or, perhaps because the people of Corinth loved wisdom, eloquence, and status while Paul championed the "foolishness of the cross."

There are any number of reasons why the Corinthians may have doubted Paul's credibility, his authority. In 2 Corinthians, while resolute, Paul writes not as a victor but as pastor with a broken heart. In Asia, where Paul likely received news of the fracture in Corinth, Paul says he was so "utterly, unbearably crushed" that he "despaired of life itself" (1:8). Twice Paul tells the Corinthians that he "does not lose heart" (4:1, 16). Why talk about "losing heart" if he hadn't in fact lost heart or was tempted to do so? Paul longed for restored affection. He begs the Corinthians to open their hearts to make room for him (6:11, 7:2). He concludes his appeal by asking, "If I love you more, am I to be loved less?" (12:15). Paul wants trust restored; he wants the breach repaired. More than anything he wants to set the Corinthians on the right path, but how?

Vacillating between begging and boasting while acknowledging that he comes close to browbeating and chest-thumping, Paul finally concludes that the lived experience of God's grace is the only testimony that stands. "You show that you are a letter of Christ," (3:3) Paul writes. And of his ministry he writes, "We have this treasure in clay jars, so that it may be made clear that this extraordinary power belongs to God and does not come from us" (4:7).

While Paul cites the pedigree of his extraordinary suffering (11:23–28) and the soaring visions and revelations given him (12:1–4), he resolves to "boast" only of his weakness "so that the power of Christ may dwell in [him]" (12:9). Paul's pride was tempered by mercy. His authority, and hence the basis of Corinthian confidence in his leadership, was a gift of grace. That gift made Paul stand upright. It gave him confidence and he hoped it would give the Corinthians confidence so that they could face head-on the challenges of faithful stewardship.

Grace tempers hubris so that we embrace our calling: "You have given them dominion over the works of your hands; you have put all things under their feet" (Ps 8:6). The dominion God shares with us is not ours to keep, which is vanity, but rather it is given to bring glory to God, "O LORD, our Sovereign, how majestic is your name in all the earth!" (Ps 8:9). Hubris tempered by grace transforms dust into vessels of hope. And hope gives us resilience to render a faithful witness. Hope thrives when we live enchanted by the awesome mystery of God's grace.

For Reflection and Discussion

1. Greg, Henry, and Sarah faced parish opposition that crossed over into their personal lives. Personal habits, compensation, and family life can be a virtual minefield for pastors and congregations alike. Where should lines be drawn? How may pride help or hinder respect for personal boundaries?

2. Elise stood for gay rights. Think about the last time you stood for principle. How may the need to be right interpose or conflict with the command to love?

3. Adam was bitterly disappointed when he was not called to his "dream" church. Is it wrong for pastors to have ambition? Why or why not?

4. Who helps you "count your days?" Who helps you maintain perspective? What has it meant to your ministry to have someone who is willing to hear your truth and tell you the truth?

5. What gives you confidence in ministry: your education, your experience, your spirituality? What erodes your confidence and what are the consequences? Have you ever been over-confident? And if so, what were the consequences? Can ministers have too little confidence? If so, what are the consequences?

6. How might enchantment with God's awesome mystery change the equation? How would you do ministry differently if your pride was tempered by humility?

CHAPTER FOUR

Hope, Enduring Fragility, and Failure

Fragile Sojourn

"If for this life only we have hoped in Christ, we are of all people most to be pitied" (1 Cor 15:19).

Life is fragile. Scientists estimate that 99.9 percent of all species that have ever existed are now extinct. That's the bad news. The good news is that the average species can expect a 10 million year run unless it meets an untimely extinction due to habitat or climate change, two typical culprits, or human interference, which is another story. Alternately, a species might be swept up in a mass extinction, which is fortunately rare—there have been only five in the last 3.5 billion years.[1]

The most famous mass extinction was 65 million years ago. The most thorough occurred 250 million years ago and is commonly known as the Great Dying. During the Great Dying the oceans' surface temperatures reached 104 degrees, killing 96 percent of all marine species. More than two-thirds of all terrestrial vertebrates became extinct. Not even the bugs were spared—57 percent of all families and 83 percent of all genera were lost. But not to worry—given time and lots of it, fragile life bounces back. In the case of the Great Dying, because so much biodiversity was lost, recovery may have taken 10 million or more years, which in earth time, is a mere chapter, perhaps two.[2]

---

1. Wikipedia, "Extinction."
2. Wikipedia, "Permian-Triassic Extinction Event."

Things fall apart. We fail. We die. That's the bad news or maybe it's just news. We are human. Or, from the gloss Genesis gives, we became aware we were created human when we "saw that the tree was good for food, and that it was a delight to the eyes, and that the tree was to be desired to make one wise" (3:6). So we ate and our "eyes were opened" and we knew that we "were naked"; we were exposed, vulnerable. We knew we were not gods or God but human.

We are born and we die. But before we die we "sweat" and "toil" and have "pangs in childbearing" and are troubled by twisted "desire," which not to say we are incapable of eating and drinking and making merry. We most certainly are and we should make merry.

I'll leave the big questions involved in all of this for others, though I do think Barth was basically right when he said that even God's "No" is God's "Yes."[3] God limits our humanity. God's "No," the fact that we die, makes way for God's "Yes," the gift of eternal life. That big frame resides behind a much smaller one that concerns me now: how do we experience endurance in our brief, fragile sojourn? And by "endure" I don't mean "endure" as in enduring a root canal or a boring opera or a long and tedious conversation with a stranger on an airplane. Rather, I mean the endurance Paul so frequently talks about when he refers to hope. I mean endurance as in "patient endurance," the kind of endurance that makes life worth living.

I want to ask how walking in wonder might change the way we endure and how wonder might help us endure with hope. To attempt an answer to that, I want to introduce three ministers, each meeting and sometimes crashing into the limits of our common humanity that test and/or inspire endurance. I want to ask how grace-inspired wonder might change the lives of the ministers I introduce. I want to ask how wonder inspires hope for the journey.

Ian

Ian pressed his back against the exam room wall, trying to make the fat rolls on his belly appear somewhat less obvious. He wasn't having much luck. The lab tech who had just taken his blood pressure said she'd be right back. His pressure read 190/110. Ian figured his stress echocardiogram might get scratched if his pressure didn't calm down. "If they hadn't crushed my arm

---

3. Barth, *Church Dogmatics* 3.1, 330ff.

with that damn mechanical cuff," Ian thought, "I'd probably be all right. How long are they going to keep me waiting?"

An older tech about Ian's age came into the room. "Mr. Sutherland, are you mad, upset, or irritated?"

"Yes."

"I'm sorry we kept you waiting."

"Well, you said to be here at four, which I was prepared to do, and then your office called and asked if I could come at three and I was here at 2:50 and I sat there for nearly an hour before I was called back."

"So, you're mad?" the tech said, forcing a smile. "I'm sorry I made you wait. I was the one who called and asked if you could come in early. It's my fault. Let me try taking your pressure again; this time in your right arm and without the mechanical cuff."

"Maybe that would help," Ian said. "The last tech almost broke my arm."

The tech finished retaking his blood pressure. "Okay, Mr. Sutherland, 168/85. Are you on any blood pressure medications? Did you take any this morning?"

"Nope. No blood pressure meds, just a statin drug and a low dose aspirin. Are they going to let me have this echo today or not?"

"We'll see. It's up to the doctor," the tech said as she closed the door.

Ian leaned back against the wall again and let out a big sigh. The pulse rate monitor dropped below 90bpm. Ian took another deep breath and let it out slowly: "Pretty cool, another 5bpm. That's still high, but I gotta have this test. My pressure was 120/80 a week ago. Today's must be white-coat syndrome, that and making me wait; too much time to think."

This was Ian's fifth echo. Like clockwork, every ten years beginning when he was thirty, except the last one was four years ago. This time was different. He'd been symptomatic, or more so than previously.

Heart disease had not been kind to Sutherland men. Ian hoped he had his mother's genes but then her father died when he was in his mid-seventies—out of the blue—died on the front porch after walking down the sidewalk to pick up the morning paper. "Maybe I won't be like that or my father. Who dies at fifty-six? But he smoked, never exercised, and was overweight."

Ian looked down at the wires strapped to his sagging chest. "How'd I get like this? I used to have a six-pack, now it looks like I'm wearing one—too many high gravity craft beers or garden variety PBR. I've got to cut back. And no more cigars, none of that—the cigars will be easy, but I do like my beer."

Dr. MacMillan bounced into the room and asked Ian how he was feeling. Ian took comfort in the fact that Dr. MacMillan was about his age, 59, balding and twenty pounds overweight. Ian smiled and said, "Let's do this," and hopped on the treadmill.

"You ride a bike don't you?" Dr. MacMillan asked, looking over the cardio tape spilling from the machine.

"Yeah. I try. Started thirty years ago. Usually I ride with friends, sometimes alone. But I prefer riding with others. It's safer."

"So, you wear a heart rate monitor when you ride?"

"Yeah. I'll go maybe thirty miles. Most of the time 130–140bpm. Might hit 160 on a hill or when we sprint the last mile."

"Probably can't do that long before going anaerobic?" Dr. Mac observed with a grin.

"Yeah. You've got that right."

"Okay, Mr. Sutherland. How are you feeling? Feeling all right? Legs all right?"

"I'm good."

"Okay, so we're going to step it up. You think you can hold 160bpm? The test is more accurate if you can hold it there for 60 seconds."

"No problem," Ian beamed, though his legs were throbbing and his breathing labored.

Dr. MacMillan stepped out of the lab while Ian stepped off the treadmill and stretched out on the exam table for the final sonogram. "Mr. Sutherland, I want you to stop breathing, hold your breath. I know your lungs are screaming otherwise, but this picture's going to be much better if you hold still."

Ian thought the tech was going to crack a rib if she pressed the camera any harder. "We're almost done. Hold your breath, one more time for me. That's it. You can sit up now."

Ian watched the video loop on the screen just to his left. "Cathump, Cathump. Cathump." Amazing. "You can get dressed. The doctor will be right in."

Dr. MacMillan studied the pulsing loop. "Well, you threw off some PVCs when we first started but once you got going they stopped. That's not unusual and that's probably what you felt when you were mowing the lawn. I wouldn't worry about it. "You see your heart at rest here," Dr. MacMillan said pointing to the gray pulsing picture. "And you see it here at 160bpm. That's a perfectly healthy heart—great blood flow. See you in a year."

"So, no restrictions?" Ian asked.

"Do what you want; just keep it legal. See you in a year."

Ian was left alone in the room with the technician. "Hey, I'm sorry if I was abrupt with you earlier. I wasn't mad at you, but the situation, that and having to be here in the first place."

"It was my fault, really," the tech smiled. "I should have waited and let you come in at your scheduled time."

"It's no bother," Ian laughed. "Do you know what my occupation is?"

"No. Tell me."

"I'm a minister. You know that church out on Elm Street?"

"Yeah, yeah. My daughter went to high school with a preacher's daughter from there. What was his name—must have been about fifteen years ago?"

"Jack Price?"

"Yeah. That's him. Nice guy."

Relieved, Ian slipped off the table. "It's been nice meeting you."

"Nice meeting you too. Have a great evening."

"You too."

Ian picked up the phone. The first call was to his wife of thirty-eight years. "Hey shug, guess what? They say I'm going to live. Got an A-plus on the test—come back in a year!"

Sabbath

If birth is a sprint, life is a marathon. Recognizing this, endurance athletes must guard against overreaching. The same is true for ministers like Ian, ministers like you and me. Fatigue is normal. We all get tired. Fifty-plus-hour work-weeks are typical; the tasks and multiple demands are oftentimes distressing. Time is seldom our own. When not working, we are always on call. When it's 2 a.m. and the phone rings, we answer. Days off and vacations are routinely scheduled around parish life. We live expecting days and weeks to bring the unexpected, all while writing weekly sermons, preparing liturgy, and managing underfunded budgets. One minute may bring joyful news of childbirth, the next the death of a beloved member. So we expect fatigue.

Overreaching is another thing. How much is too much? What are the signs? Ian, like most of us, pushed himself. His heart told him to slow down, but rather than listening to his heart he kept plugging along. What should we look for and more importantly how do we respond to fatigue so that we are able to bounce back?

The primary source of energy for physical activity is glucose. Glucose is produced by glycogen stored in muscle tissues. When we exercise glycogen stores increase and hence we have greater endurance. But as every runner or bike rider or swimmer will tell you, we can overdo it. And when we do, when we don't allow sufficient recovery time, when we overreach, muscle tissue breaks down and fatigue sets in.

Fatigue may also set in when we overstress mitochondrial capacity. Mitochondria use oxygen and remove cellular waste. When we overdo it, mitochondrial capacity can be exceeded. Likewise, lactic acid accumulates when we exercise. When a muscle is overworked a backflow of blood rushing to the muscle inhibits lactic acid from being removed. The result is the burning sensation we feel when our muscles no longer contract. We bonk.

The same thing happens when we lose more fluids than we drink. We dehydrate. Go long enough dehydrated and our body revolts—fatigue, dizziness, dry mouth, rapid pulse, cramps, headache. Our bodies are not stupid but sometimes we are. We overreach. We burn out. So, what's the solution? First, recognize we're not Superman or Superwoman. We are human. We are limited, but God is gracious. God invites us to rest, to recover, to keep Sabbath.

The physical effects of overdoing exercise are mirrored by the effects of overdoing ministry. As Amy Fryholm observes, "Being a pastor is bad for your health."[4] Clergy have higher than normal rates of obesity, arthritis, depression, heart problems, high blood pressure, diabetes, and stress. One study found that 40 percent of United Methodist clergy in North Carolina were obese, a figure 11 percent higher than the state average and 14 percent higher than the national average. Even more alarming, the same study found that while Methodist clergy who enrolled in wellness training showed gains in four out of five metabolic measures, stress levels were not decreased. Rae Jean Proeschold-Bell, lead researcher for the project, said if she could make one change it would be to "shift the way that congregants think about their pastor. I would want them to think about the pastor as a whole person. Not as a person on a pedestal dedicated to serving them, but

---

4. Frykholm, "Fit for Ministry," 22.

as a human being with flaws and graces."[5] I would add: although we may never ask to be put on one, pastors need to get off the pedestal. If we don't act like real human beings, how can our congregations regard us otherwise? Endurance requires clear-headed, clear-hearted acknowledgment that we are human. We are limited.

Recognizing our limits means allowing time for rest and recovery. Because our times are so often not our own, pastors need to be intentional about setting boundaries. If you are like me, you probably try to schedule a day off and keep it, most weeks two days, back to back. I often find that there are times when that is impossible—the funeral that could only be scheduled for Friday, the wedding on Saturday night, a congregation-wide event on Sunday evening. When that happens, I force myself to make up the lost time the following week. I take an afternoon off and don't apologize for it. I need rest. I need time for recovery.

Protracted constant availability takes a toll both physically and spiritually. When I push too hard, I develop feelings of resentment. I sometimes feel depressed or just plain tired and then I am of no help to anyone. I find that I must schedule vacation and study leave the same way I schedule parish life. And when I'm on vacation, I don't check my email. I ditch my cell phone. Okay, so maybe I don't always ditch the phone, but I do make contingency plans so family vacations are not cut short. I also ask for help, something that doesn't come naturally to me. After all, I'm a helper. Why should I have to ask for help?

Most personnel committees are more compassionate than I've expected, but they haven't and can't and don't know my needs unless I voice them. Even the ox is entitled to grain (1 Cor 9:9). I've learned to ask for help. When I've tried to appear invincible, who's to think otherwise? Grace does not make us invincible. Grace allows us to be the human beings we are. Grace allows rest, recovery, Sabbath. Ask for it. Expect it. Enjoy it.

Virginia

Virginia stared at the falling snow. Ordinarily she liked snow but all she could think about was the crummy planning meeting the night before. Virginia, thirty-five, and in her second call, didn't blame the planning committee members. They were doing the best they could. She was doing the best she could. Everybody was worried about the same thing—declining

---

5. Ibid., 26.

membership. Thirty years ago worship averaged one hundred in Virginia's now struggling church. When attendance hit fifty, the church was yoked with a nearby sister church so both could afford one full-time pastor. Virginia knew that when she accepted the call three years earlier. She thought she could make a difference. She loved the challenge and was full of ideas. Virginia hadn't counted on one thing: no one had moved into her small town in thirty years. Traffic flowed one way—out, a decline of more than 20 percent in the last twenty years.

Virginia's church, founded in 1840, would celebrate its 175th anniversary in two years. Virginia wondered if she'd stick around that long. It was a tough call. Not that the people weren't salt of the earth—they were. And not that there weren't problems typical of small churches—there were. Something more troubling nagged at Virginia as she watched the falling snow. Maybe she was wrong for the job, maybe she wasn't as missional or emergent as everyone said. Maybe God had other plans.

Virginia looked glumly at a stack of books on her desk—five steps, seven practices, ten keys. What was it about experts and numbers? If growing a church was that easy, why couldn't she do it? And why after their own success did the experts leave their churches, publish books, and ride the circuit selling their wares? She had followed the steps and the practices and the keys and there was precious little to show for it other than her own disappointment and sagging spirits among her beleaguered people. Secretly she wished one of the experts would parachute into her small town and try plying their cookbook solutions and see how they fared.

The phone rang. It was Harriet Johnson. She was in tears. Her husband Marvin fell on an icy patch and banged his head. The ER doc thought Marvin was going to be okay but would she mind dropping by the hospital? Virginia hung up the phone, pulled on her parka and boots, and headed out into the falling snow.

Footprints Unseen

When I graduated from seminary I wandered into the bookstore and purchased a book, *My Pastoral Record*. The leather-bound volume runs nearly five hundred pages. I'm guessing the publishers expected that purchasers would stay in ministry for a very long time. National averages trend otherwise. Ministry is often not what we expect. When I look back over my own record there are plenty of sermons but more funerals than baptisms.

With Virginia I've stared at falling snow more than once and wondered, what's the point? I've read many of the books she read with their keys and practices and essentials for "successful" ministry and worried with her that something must be wrong with me because successes have often been less than stellar, if by "success" we mean more baptisms than funerals, more new members than transfers to the inactive roll. I have trudged out into the snow more times than I care to count from a sense of duty rather than expectant wonder. I'm not particularly proud of that, but if I'm honest I must admit that I've often labored with more worry than wonder—worry about meeting a budget, worry about growing a church, worry about keeping the doors open and the light bill paid.

As I imagine you have, I've questioned my ability, my faith, my leadership, my hope. With the psalmist I have also questioned God, "Has God forgotten to be gracious? Has he in anger shut up his compassion?" (77:9) With the psalmist, I have longed for days gone by when "doing church" seemed easier.

Since my ordination, the denomination I serve has lost one-third of its members. I have longed for bygone days when ministry was different. Experts tell us that God is doing a new thing; a new, more missional church is emerging. Perhaps we should simply wait and see. I don't profess to know what God is doing, but I do confess that thirty-plus years of ministry has taught me that faithful ministry can't be measured by numbers, declining or rising ones. Faithful ministry is measured by our hope in the kingdom of God, by the One who is at work among us doing far more than we can ask or imagine. Faithful ministry endures when we walk in wonder and act in faithful response to the claims, demands, and promises of the gospel.

Large forces shape every context for ministry—population shifts, job loss, economic development or a lack thereof. But a larger force still shapes ministry—"the God who works wonders" (Ps 77:14).

The "God who works wonders" inspires hope, not the faint images we see in filled pews or well-funded budgets, but hope in the One who moves mighty in our midst. The psalmist never tires of recalling God's creative power: "When the waters saw you, O God, when the waters saw you they were afraid; the very deep trembled" (77:16). The deep that "trembled and shook" made a "way through the sea," God's path "through the mighty waters." And yet, and this for me is the great surprise of wondrous grace, God's "footprints were *unseen*." What was seen was "the hand of Moses and Aaron" or perhaps just their footprints, or with Virginia, tracks in fallen snow. Patient endurance comes when we follow "the God who works wonders," the One whose footprints are unseen, the One who inspires hope.

Nate and Dr. Hightower

Nate Jackson was flattered when the regional council executive called to ask him to serve on an administrative review committee. The council, charged with oversight of 125 churches, had received disturbing complaints about the Rev. Dr. Jacob Hightower, senior pastor of a flagship church in a major city. With rumors and conflict swirling, the 1,600-member church had recently voted to retain their long-time pastor. It was a split decision. Sixty percent thought Dr. Hightower deserved a second chance. Forty percent said it was time for him to go. The exec explained that the council had a responsibility to hear the minority and determine if the vote should be sustained. Rev. Jackson was twenty-seven years old and new to the council. He did not know Dr. Hightower and figured wiser heads thought he would bring an unbiased opinion to the investigation. When Nate agreed to the executive's request he had little idea what he was in for. Seminary had hardly prepared him for what he was about to experience.

Nate grabbed a quick bite after worship and told his wife he'd be home by noon Monday. The three-hour drive to Dr. Hightower's church gave Nate time to think. The profile emailed by the council exec was impressive. Dr. Hightower's resumé read like a "who's who": a Princeton graduate, doctoral studies in Europe, various civic awards, multiple publications in prestigious journals, and a sterling denominational service record. Dr. Hightower, now age sixty-two, had risen through the ranks like a meteor. He had landed at First Church before his fortieth birthday and from all indications the church flourished during his twenty-two years there.

On the gray winter day, driving by vast, fallow fields, Nate's mind wandered. His heart raced. "What had gone wrong? How could a guy like Dr. Hightower lose it? Had he lost it? If it could happen to him, it could happen to anybody."

Nate arrived at the church at 4 p.m. and was greeted by Grady Todd, chair of the administrative review committee. Rev. Todd was affable but a no-nonsense guy. He wasted little time hustling Nate along with six others into a meeting room. After coffee and prayer Grady briefed the committee, explaining that they would work in teams of two. "Your job is to listen. Allegations of sexual misconduct, alcohol abuse, and neglect of pastoral care and responsibility are flying all around this place. There are probably fifty or sixty people who want to speak to us today. We will divide into four teams. The members will come in groups of four or five and spend thirty minutes with one of our teams. Make notes. We expect to see everyone over the next two hours and then at seven p.m. we will interview Dr. Hightower. Afterward we will meet and debrief. Any questions?"

Nate was no longer flattered. This was serious business.

The interviews were painful. Some First Church members were clearly hurt and deeply disappointed by Dr. Hightower's behavior and thought he should go. Some were angry at the administrative review committee. They thought Dr. Hightower was being railroaded. Others were resigned. They weren't convinced that all of the allegations were true and didn't want to believe them true, but so much damage had been done and so much confidence had been eroded they thought Dr. Hightower should resign. They weren't out to get him. They just wanted their church back.

By seven everyone who wanted to speak had spoken. Nate was weary. The whole team was weary. It was time for Dr. Hightower. Grady suggested a break before proceeding. Nate was glad for the break but dreaded what was next.

Dr. Hightower was not what Nate expected. He had imagined a vigorous, attractive, well-spoken sixty-two-year old at the top of his game. Instead, Dr. Hightower looked bloated. His cheeks were puffy and red. The dark blue suit he was wearing was ill-fitting. What disturbed Nate most was Dr. Hightower's eyes. They flitted about the room landing nowhere in particular. But there was also defiance in his expression. When he spoke his hands jabbed the air. He mostly talked about the past, his achievements, his record, the long hours he had put in for over forty years in ministry. The allegations against him were falsehoods. But all of his bluster could not erase the conclusion that weighed heavily in the room. Dr. Hightower was his own worst accuser.

With the interview over, Grady offered prayer for Dr. Hightower, cleared his throat and explained that the administrative review committee would report in two weeks. Dr. Hightower shook Grady's hand and left the room.

The evidence was overwhelming. Despite the congregation's slim vote of confidence, the committee agreed that Dr. Hightower should be removed from office. Grady thanked the committee members and asked them to prepare for the council meeting in two weeks. The long drive home the next morning gave Nate plenty of time to think. "So this is church? What will I say if they ask me to speak?"

Regional council meetings were part family reunion and part boring business. They were usually held in big churches to accommodate the three hundred-plus voting members. On the day appointed for the review committee's report, Nate wore his best suit, actually his only suit, a gray pen-stripe. The suit made him look older, or so he thought. Maybe he wouldn't be asked to speak. Maybe it would be an up and down vote. Nate was wrong. When he arrived in the narthex, Grady cornered him. "Look, this is a big deal. While it's not a trial, the council wants to hear from all eight of us. So, be ready." Nate's head began to spin.

When the order of the day came, Nate assembled at the podium with Grady and the others. They each spoke in turn. When Nate began, his voice cracked. "You know, I'm just a guy like the rest of you. Nobody wants to be standing where we're standing today. Nobody wants to point an accusing finger. We all have clay feet. And what Dr. Hightower has done or is rumored to have done is not pleasant. The truth is it could be any of us, but I have come to the same difficult conclusion as the other committee members. None of us wants to make this decision, but we see no other course of action." And with that, Nate sat down.

When the vote was taken, it was unanimous. Dr. Hightower was removed from office.

Friendship

Ministry is inherently isolating. We can be around people all day long and feel alone. You have probably known, or known of, ministers like Dr. Hightower who have ended in catastrophic failure. Or maybe, like Nate, you have watched helplessly as a beloved colleague became his own worst enemy. What do you want to say before it goes all wrong? And is what we say advice that we follow?

Like Jacob, I have been tempted and I have fallen to the temptation to simply become The Pastor. I have allowed myself to simply hold an office. I have been The Teacher, The Administrator, The Boss, The Planner, The Organizer, The Head Cheerleader, The Servant, The Prophet, The Wounded Healer. With young Nate and Jacob in his better moments, I have wondered how my ministry might have been differently shaped if I hadn't acted as if I was alone.

Ministers have more agency than we often realize. "For freedom Christ has set us free" (Gal 5:1). Freedom is not an opportunity for self-indulgence," but rather the promise to give ourselves "through love" to others (Gal 5:13). Genuine love does not mean we become cardboard figures. People don't want that anyway.

Becoming the person God creates us to be requires friendship. It requires play. And play is a function of wonder. Play is delighting in others not because they are a means to an end but because friendship is an end in itself. Friendship creates space for wonder. And wonder energizes the soul. Wonder allows us to find joy in the other, joy that refreshes us in the midst of our brief, fragile sojourn. We endure.

When I moved to Mobile my days were busy. I had my hands full. And I ran like crazy. Truth be told, twelve years later, I still do. Over the course of my first months in Mobile, a man named Marion Adams used to drop by my office on Sunday mornings thirty minutes or so before things heated up. Marion was a retired businessman and a life-long member. He never stayed in my office long. Most conversations began the same way, with Marion asking me, "How are you doing?" Marion didn't quiz me about how things were going with my new staff or with a major capital campaign we were undertaking. He didn't ask about my plans or vision. He simply wanted to know how *I* was doing.

Marion died a few years ago. While visiting with his family to plan his funeral service, I mentioned his Sunday morning visits and told his family how much they had meant to me. Marion was a man in whom there was no guile. His wife, Ann, was pleased. "Oh, you know Marion. For as long as I can remember, he did that with all of our ministers. He wanted all of you to know how much we cared about you as human beings. That was Marion."

I thank God for Marion and for people like him, men and women who care about their pastors as human beings. Marion helped me realize the freedom for which Christ has set us free, free to love and serve God fully as the human beings we are. Ministers don't have to be alone. With friends, we can serve freely and fully with the "flaws and graces" we have and are.

"I praise you, for I am fearfully and wonderfully made" (Ps 139:14).

God created us with a remarkable capacity to bounce back. Our bodies no less than our spirits are resilient and are made more so when we run with faith, when we are sustained by friendship, when we endure with hope. God also loves us with perfect love, love that enables us to live not only with our "flaws and graces," but also with the ambiguities we daily meet, a topic for the next chapter. The steadfast love of God endures forever. And because it does we endure with hope.

For Reflection and Discussion

1. Ian's story: When was the last time you had your heart checked, your blood pressure, your cholesterol? When was the last time you had a complete physical? How would you rate your physical health? What role does physical health play in your capacity to do ministry?

2. Virginia's story: Ministry is contextual, local. And every context, every locale has a peculiar history. Large forces shape every context—population shifts, economic development or the lack thereof. Think about Virginia and her context for ministry. How should she measure success? Is church growth the be-all and end-all of ministry? What are the measures of faithful ministry?

3. Jacob's story: Ministers fail. Ministers sin. When have you been your own worst enemy? When was the last time you failed or flopped in ministry and how did you bounce back?

4. What role does fatigue play in your ability to stay the course and finish the race? Loneliness and isolation contribute to fatigue. How has friendship influenced your capacity to do ministry?

5. What do you do for fun? How do you play? What contributes to your rest and recovery? What brings you joy? When are you "lost in wonder and love"?

6. Consider a time in ministry when you met adversity. How did hope influence your decisions and the path you took? How would you describe the difference between hope and wishful thinking? What role might wonder play in how you respond to adversity?

7. Name some of the personal, institutional, and social limits you face in ministry. Are limits always "bad"? How might embracing your limits free you to do ministry differently, in hope rather than despair, in responsibility rather than retreat?

CHAPTER FIVE

Steadfast Love, Reframing Ambiguity

Ambiguity

THE EARTH MOVES. ROCKS break. Is anything fixed, stable, permanent, eternal (Parmenides, ca. 515–450 BCE)? Or is everything flux and flow (Heraclitus, ca. 535–475 BCE)?

Ambiguity. We circle around the stuff of reality, or "what is" and see differently—no change, all change, maybe some change. Although it is uncertain that Parmenides and Heraclitus ever crossed the Aegean to discuss their differences, their perspectives reflect the ambiguity inherent in "what is." "What is" is not self-evident. There is more than one way of naming or seeing "what is" or even agreeing "what is." Moreover, how we see or name "what is" is framed by our respective points of view, which have many origins.

A fast moving train appears "fast" to an observer standing trackside, close enough to feel the ground tremble and air pulse. To a commercial pilot cruising at 32,000 feet, the train appears to creep along at a snail's pace. Similarly, a passenger on the "fast" moving train who is late arriving for an important meeting may feel she will never reach her destination, while two lovers in the seat opposite her wish the moment would never end. How we frame "what is" gives credence to the expression that "perception is reality" or almost, for "what is" is not simply a matter of framing. Moving trains arrive when they arrive.

Back to a moving earth. . . . The earth's crust we stand upon, the lithosphere (literally: "stone ball") floats on something akin to a sea, the asthenosphere (literally: "weak ball"). Over geologic time, the lithosphere, which has enjoyed its present configuration for merely one-tenth of earth's history, has undergone multiple formations and is still moving. One example: North America and Europe drift apart about one and a half inches a year, at roughly the pace fingernails grow.[1]

Given our infinitesimally brief sojourn relative to geological time, the ground beneath us appears fixed, solid as a rock, though when tectonic plates slide by one another or pass beneath or rise above one another the resulting jolt shocks belief that there is "nothing new under the sun" (Eccl 1:9). And if tectonic plates did not move, if the earth stood still, forever and for all time, we wouldn't be here. Thank goodness the sea floor renews itself every 250 million years, otherwise the ground we stand upon would indeed be "solid as a rock," only we would not be here to enjoy the ride. Without movement, apart from breaking rock, there would be nothing we call "life," no singing birds, no slithering worms, no crashing waves or beating human hearts. Without change there would be stability, all of the stability of Mars, but no you, or me, or singing birds, just one solid mass like Mars, which, so far as we know, remains lifeless.

What does it mean to live on an ever-changing earth? For starters, and this is a big start, there is more than one way of seeing "what is." A moving earth means ambiguity. A moving earth gives rise to life, growth, change, newness, and also love, joy, hope, wonder. But likewise, a moving earth means decay, destruction, death, and may give rise to despair, suffering, nihilism, a different sort of non-life.

So, what does a moving earth have to do with anything? Everything! I don't wish to wander down Leibniz's "best-of-all-possible-worlds" road except to say that, yes, we can imagine a world where buildings don't collapse, or one where tsunamis don't sweep away thousands—such a world is imaginable; only not open to investigation. We are stuck with the world we have. And it moves. Hence, ambiguity, which may sound like an argument for freedom, "the necessary condition" for life as we know it—not fixed but changing, not predictably planned but occasionally maddeningly random, inexplicable, wild even. I don't wish to argue that this is the "best of all possible worlds," only that this is the world we have. And the world we have gives us pause to wonder: What's it all about? Why are we here? What, if anything, holds the world together or tears it apart?

---

1. Bryson, *A Short History of Nearly Everything*, 229.

You don't have to ride out a hurricane on board a sixty-five-foot sail boat to realize that life is tumultuous. To be sure, storms don't blow every day. The uncertainty would drive even the best sailors among us to the brink of insanity. I'm glad most days for "fair winds and following seas." While I've not ridden out a hurricane at sea, I have twice boarded up my 100-year-old house in the path of Hurricanes Ivan and Katrina, and prayed for a house to wake up in the next day.

Most days I expect something bordering on *Groundhog Day*—the return of the same. I like routine. It's not that I am risk averse (a topic for coming chapters), but I do enjoy waking up knowing that there will be water for a shower and electricity for hot tea. I'm with Parmenides and Ecclesiastes on that. But when life is too predictable, I grow antsy for diversion. And sometimes diversion finds me in the random, unexpected, routine-breaking things that happen—the sewer line to the fellowship hall backs up after a four-inch, thirty-minute rain and there's not only a royal mess to clean up, but several hundred hungry homeless people who won't have breakfast; Mrs. Smith phones to say her seventy-five-year-old husband had a heart attack and now faces a triple bypass; Mr. Jones stops by and sobs that his wife of thirty years has left him; Mrs. Thomas emails that she's moving and won't be able to finish her term as chair of the Mission Committee that is about to launch a major initiative to Africa; the Office Manager reports a broken copier, and what about the bulletin due in two days; a second staff member phones in sick; my daughter calls announcing that she's expecting her third child; the news ticker on my computer screen flashes that the US has just bombed Syria—all this over three days. Okay, where do I start?

We never know what a day will bring—chores to be sure, mundane routines like brushing teeth or brewing tea, but there is always the possibility of the unpredictable, unanticipated, unexplained, unaccounted for, unmanaged stuff of life. The unexpected might not be earth-shattering but just enough surprise or uncertainty to make the day interesting, confounding, curious, but also liveable. Without the prospect of change, whether growth or decay, there is little by way of what we know as joy, or newness, or hope, or steadfast love.

How we frame our days makes all of the difference. There is more than one way of seeing "what is." And how shall we see?

Time itself is not unambiguous. The past is always changing, never fully past, no more so than the future is fully present or simply "tomorrow" or a long way off. The past tugs on the soul—regret, remorse, nostalgia, wisdom from lessons learned—all of which impinges on what we name Now. But the future no less than the past draws the soul—things hoped for, not yet, anticipated, dreamed, imagined. The past is never completely past, no more so than the future is fully present—ambiguity.

The Potter's Spinning Planet

Is anything unambiguous? Let's hope so. "Nothing in all creation will be able to separate us from the love of God in Christ Jesus our Lord" (Rom 8:39). Speaking of permanence, durability, that's one thing, foundational for everything else that we can or should or may always depend on—God's enduring love. "The steadfast love of the LORD never ceases; his mercies never come to an end; [and here is the surprise] they are *new* every morning" (Lam 3:19; emphasis mine).

How can God's love be "new"? Isn't it always the same? God's love can be new because God "gives life to the dead and calls into existence the things that do not exist" (Rom 4:17). God's love can be new because God changes God's mind (Jer 18:5ff.). The Potter is at his wheel. The earth moves. Rocks break; the stone is rolled away.

"See, I am making all things new" (Rev 21:5). Notice, not "all new things," but "all things *new*." The Potter repairs the broken, reshapes the malformed, and sometimes starts all over again—in short, the Potter makes all things new.

"I am about to do a new thing; now it springs forth, do you not perceive it?" (Isa 43:19). Well, frankly, not always. Most days what I see is all there is. I cannot see the new thing God is doing. I see ambiguity while fearing those pesky "unknown unknowns" that so plagued Donald Rumsfeld. Even when I think I've seen all there is to see, I am surprised. Say you're planning a trip. You pack your bags—change of clothes, socks, shoes, your blood pressure medicine—off you go, only to arrive without your belt, or toothbrush, or rain coat. You thought about the coat but decided your bag was already full. Who knew it would rain?

More seriously, you planned for a board meeting to discuss buying a property next door to your church (something I did while writing this book). You considered everything, or thought you did—environmental and engineering studies, financing, oversight committee, and a papered up contract. The building next door was rundown, unoccupied and compromised the view of your building, not to mention the fire-hazard created by the vacancy. So you think, "Buy it and tear it down." But not so fast—someone else on your board suggests another path, a different vision: "Let's buy the building, tear down part of it, rehab the rest, and lease it, generating a long-term revenue stream. We could do a lot of good for ministry and mission with an income like that."

What we see is all there is, or almost. There is always more than one point of view. And even when there are multiple points of view, unknown unknowns remain. Even a "team of rivals" cannot see all there is. And thank God for that. There's no telling what we would do or not do if we achieved perfect harmony. Remember the Tower of Babel? We might also miss what God is actually up to, the new thing God is doing.

Seeing around—ambiguity—can be bane or blessing. If I could see around the next curve in the road I likely would not take it if I knew a big truck was crossing the center line. Then again, if I stopped and turned around, I might miss the beautiful vista that waits beyond. Our response to ambiguity may arrest action and thereby avoid trouble but it may as well arrest surprise or joy itself.

A moving earth requires both due diligence and the acceptance of certain uncertainty otherwise known as risk. Jesus says due diligence is required of disciples—"Which of you, intending to build a tower, does not first sit down and estimate the cost, to see whether he has enough to complete it?" (Luke 14:28) But Jesus also throws caution to the wind—"Whoever comes to me and does not hate father and mother, wife and children, brothers and sister, yes even life itself, cannot be my disciple. Whoever does not carry the cross and follow me cannot be my disciple" (Luke 14:26).

Jesus invites us to walk diligently and freely amid unknown unknowns. Such walking would be utter foolishness, nonsense even, if we walked alone or walked only so long as we anticipated every bump or curve or problem or promise in advance—and we can't. Walking into unknown unknowns requires more than nerves of steel, though that helps. Following demands, or rather is grounded in, the steadfast love of the Lord whose mercies are new every morning. Following is made possible by the One who is making all things new on an earth that moves. Because the Potter is at his wheel, ambiguity can be reframed.

"I can do all things through him who strengthens me" (Phil 4:13). Notice that the "I can do" is premised upon "the Lord" who provides strength. I'll have more to say about leading and following in the next chapters, but let me anticipate what I will say there by saying here that resilience or the "I can do" is framed by Christ, by God's steadfast love.

Bouncing back from storms, curves, falls, stupidity, or plain old sin is not a brush-the-dust-off-your-pants-and-keep-moving affair. True grit takes us only so far on a moving earth. Stronger stuff is needed to keep "pressing on toward the upward calling of God in Christ" (Phil 3:14). Yes, there is faith; however, faith is not faith in itself, but faith in the One who is shaping the moving earth in ways beyond our asking or imagining. Ambiguity is reframed when we are moved to wonder by the steadfast love of God, when we are made new by the mercies of God. Reframing is not automatic but more of a dance, an event, a happening. When the Potter turns us, the world changes because we are changed. We see differently. We are made new. We are transformed by steadfast love and "what is" is newly made.

"What is" can be variously defined. Wonder, grounded in and inspired by the steadfast love of God, reframes not only what we see but also shapes the witness we give. Let me share two compelling examples.

Dietrich Bonhoeffer

On a gray Monday morning, April 9, 1945, Dietrich Bonhoeffer was summoned from his Flossenbürg cell by the Gestapo and ordered to disrobe. With five coconspirators, including Admiral Wilhelm Canaris, head of German Military Intelligence and his deputy, General Hans Oster, the thirty-nine-year-old Lutheran pastor and theologian was led to the gallows and hung. His corpse, piled with the others, was burned.

The day before his execution, Bonhoeffer led morning worship. The service was held in a Schönberg schoolhouse, some fifty miles from Flossenbürg. It was Low Sunday. The text was from the prophet Isaiah: "With his stripes we are healed" (53:5). When the service ended, other prisoners wanted to smuggle Bonhoeffer to their room so that he could hold services there, but before the request could be fulfilled, two civilians entered the room and called out: "Prisoner Bonhoeffer, get ready and come with us." Bonhoeffer gathered his things, including his volume of Plutarch. In large letters with a blunt pencil Bonhoeffer wrote his name and address in the front, middle, and back of the book and left it behind as if to say, "I was here." Before entering the transport to Flossenbürg, Bonhoeffer asked

Captain Payne Best to remember him to his friend Bishop George Bell. According to Best, these were Bonhoeffer's last words to him: "This is the end—for me the beginning of life."[2]

Two weeks later, Allied Forces entered Flossenbürg, and in three weeks Hitler was dead. It would be June before Bonhoeffer's twenty-year-old fiancée, Maria von Wedemeyer, learned of his death. His parents heard the news the following month.

Ten years later the camp doctor of Flossenbürg recalled the morning of April 9:

> Through the half-open door in one room of the huts I saw Pastor Bonhoeffer, before taking off his prison garb, kneeling on the floor praying fervently to his God.... At the place of execution, he again said a short prayer and then climbed the steps to the gallows, brave and composed. His death ensued after a few seconds. In the almost fifty years that I worked as a doctor, I have hardly ever seen a man die so entirely submissive to the will of God.[3]

Despite this and other accounts, Bonhoeffer did not wish to be remembered as a hero or martyr. "The ultimate question for a responsible man to ask is not how he is to extricate himself heroically from the affair, but how the coming generation is to live. It is only from this question, with its responsibility towards history, that fruitful solutions can come, even if for the time being they are humiliating."[4] From Bonhoeffer's perspective our responsibility for history "depends on a God who demands responsible action in a bold venture of faith, and who promises forgiveness and consolation to the man who becomes a sinner in that venture."[5]

Bonhoeffer's embrace of the historical ambiguity he faced and his acceptance of his role in two conspiracies to assassinate Hitler were not grounded in heroism or a wish for martyrdom, but rather in his confidence in and his awe before the steadfast love of God who forgives sinners. As letters from his Tegel Prison cell in Berlin bear witness, that stance was not reached absent homesickness, acedia, self-pity, plans for escape, and, if briefly, thoughts of suicide itself. God's steadfast love did not erase ambiguity for Bonhoeffer, nor does it for us, but it does allow us to endure and see beyond ambiguity.

2. Bethge, *Dietrich Bonhoeffer*, 830.
3. Ibid, 830–31.
4. Bonhoeffer, *Letters and Papers from Prison*, 7.
5. Ibid, 6.

STEADFAST LOVE, REFRAMING AMBIGUITY

In 1942, five months prior to his arrest, Bonhoeffer wrote a Christmas letter to his brother-in-law, Hans von Dohnanyi, and to his friends, Hans Oster and Eberhard Bethge. The letter, titled "After Ten Years" and published as the prologue to *Letters and Papers From Prison*, anticipates what Bonhoeffer would name his "boundary" or "borderline" situation, which, in Bethge's words, led him "to abandon all outward and inward security."[6]

"Boundary" and "borderline" aptly describe ambiguity. As someone has observed, it's not heights that frighten us, but edges. Borderlines and boundaries are where things get "fuzzy," both internally and externally. Bonhoeffer expressed this "fuzziness" in his Christmas letter when he asked "whether there have ever before in human history been people with *so little ground under their feet*—people to whom every available alternative seemed equally intolerable, repugnant, and futile?" (emphasis mine).[7]

Given the moving earth beneath our feet, Bonhoeffer wondered who stood fast—reasonable people, fanatics, people of conscience, those obedient to duty, those who assert freedom, or perhaps the privately virtuous. He answered that the only one who stands fast is the "man whose final standard is not his reason, his principles, his conscience, his freedom, or his virtue, but who is ready to sacrifice all this when he is called to obedient and responsible action in faith and in exclusive allegiance to God—the responsible man, who tries to make his whole life an answer to the question and call of God."[8] We stand upon a moving earth when we hold fast to God, or rather, when God holds fast to us; ambiguity is met by faith.

"I believe," Bonhoeffer wrote to his friends, "that God can and will bring good out of evil, even out of the greatest evil. . . . I believe that God will give us all the strength we need to help us to resist in all times of distress. *But he never gives it in advance*, lest we should rely on ourselves and not on him alone" (emphasis mine).[9] God's steadfast love overcomes ambiguity, but not without a fight and at times and under certain circumstances it may even appear absent or weak or beyond faith's grasp. Few places in Bonhoeffer's work better attest to the spinning, whirling dance of faith than his poem, "Who Am I?"

> Who am I? They often tell me I would step from my cell's confinement
> calmly, cheerfully, firmly,

---

6. Bethge, *Dietrich Bonhoeffer*, 700.
7. Ibid., 3.
8. Ibid., 5.
9. Ibid., 11.

like a squire from his country house.
....

They also tell me I would bear the days of misfortune
equably, smilingly, proudly,
like one accustomed to win.

Am I then all that which other men tell of?
Or am I only what I know of myself,
restless and longing and sick, like a bird in a cage,
struggling for breath, as though hands were compressing my throat,
....

weary and empty at praying, at thinking, at making
faint, and ready to say farewell to it all?

Who am I? This or the other?
Am I one person today, and tomorrow another?
Am I both at once? A hypocrite before others,
and before myself a contemptibly woebegone weakling?
Or is something within me still like a beaten army,
fleeing in disorder from victory already achieved?

Who am I? They mock me, these lonely questions of mine.
Whoever I am, thou knowest, O God, I am thine.[10]

Is anything unambiguous? To the eyes of faith, yes—the steadfast love of God—not faith itself, not calmness, or cheerfulness, or courage even. We stand on the steadfast love of God or nothing at all. Ambiguity is never entirely arrested or removed, but it may be reframed when newly seen in the light cast by God's steadfast love. That, I am convinced, is a wondrous thing.

Kou Homsombath

I want to tell you about a man whose circumstances could not have been more ambiguous and yet he not only lived to tell about it, but gave praise to God and brought blessing to the people of God.

---

10. Ibid., 347–48.

STEADFAST LOVE, REFRAMING AMBIGUITY

Kou Homsombath was a thirty-two-year-old French-trained telegraph operator in the Royalist Army of Laos when Pathet Lao, backed by the Soviet Union and the Vietnam People's Army, overthrew the Laotian government, forcing King Savang Vatthana to abdicate on December 2, 1975. Civil war followed, claiming as many as 70,000 Laotian lives. After signing agreements with Vietnam to station forces and appoint overseers, Kaysone Phomvihane renamed the former French Colony and US ally the Lao People's Democratic Republic. Unrest continued, especially between Hmong rebels and the Vietnam People's Army in collaboration with Phomyihane's regime. By some counts, one-fourth or 100,000 Hmong were killed. Thousands of other Laotians were rounded up, including Kou Homsombath, who, in October 1977, was captured by the communists and moved three hundred miles north of his home, Vientiane, where he was forced to work in a prisoner of war camp as a farmer.

The following year Kou was transferred closer to home. He was determined to be reunited with his wife, Vongphet, and five young children. One May night in 1978, during a driving rain storm, Kou managed to escape and returned to his family in Vientiane. That same night the family stole a boat and fled across the mile-wide rain swollen Mekong River. The river crossing took nearly an hour. When the Homosombaths reached the Thai border cold and wet, they hid among weeds. During the night, the family saw other escapees shot by the Thai police. When morning came they were arrested. After being jailed for nineteen days, during which they had to beg for food, the Homsombaths were sent to Nong Khai, a refugee camp about six kilometers from Bangkok. The camp housed 40,000 people.

The family of seven lived in a nine-by-nine-foot hut where they slept side by side. Vilalilach, the Homsombath's eleven-year-old daughter, took in sewing to raise money for scarce supplies. Stabbings, shootings, theft, and rape were ever present reminders of the perils they faced. There was no work for Kou, who spent most of his time sitting—too upset to eat or sleep. And so it would be for the next sixteen months until Church World Services, working in cooperation with five Presbyterian churches in Hancock County, Illinois, arranged for the Homsombaths' resettlement. The Homsombaths were among 250,000 Laotians to find a new home in America in the years following the Vietnam War.

My wife and I, along with nearby Presbyterian friends, met the Homsombaths for the first time at the St. Louis airport on October 5, 1979. After a four-hour drive home, we learned of their amazing and perilous story through broken English and French, and not a few pictures drawn on a tablet. The next morning we woke up to sounds in the kitchen—Vongphet had made a huge pot of rice. Kou and the older children were outside raking newly fallen October leaves. We were humbled by their eager expressions of gratitude and awed by the enormity of it all—one family's plight swept up in the wages of war, ambiguity, and survival.

After a week with us, our church rented a house for the Homsombaths three blocks away from our house. Church members went to work providing clothes, household furnishings, food, a bank account, language classes, and no small measure of daily kindnesses. Though language was a barrier and no doubt sober Presbyterian worship was strange, Kou and Vongphet, with their children in tow, never missed a Sunday. "Mr. Kou," as we called him, sat in worship with studied patience. The look on his face was at once curious and familiar as if to say, "I understand."

Kou found employment in a nearby candle factory, while Vongphet worked in a nursing home. By the end of October, Kou's brother and nephew joined the family. The following March Kou's brother moved to Beaverton, Oregon in pursuit of a marriage proposal from an extended family member.

In mid-April, Kou's wife moved to Texas. Kou told me that he and his family wanted to stay, but when Vongphet left she insisted that they either come to her or they would never see her again. Kou hugged me with tears in his eyes as we parted company that night.

The Homsombaths left the next day, refusing to take what had been given them, partly out of appreciation, partly from the cost of shipping. They insisted that our twenty-month-old daughter, Meredith, keep the children's toys. They left as they came, with little more than the clothes they wore. Actually they left with more than that—they left encouraged, uplifted, embraced by the people of God who had welcomed them to their new home.

A year and a half later, we received a Christmas card from the Homsombaths. By then we had a new addition to our household, our son, Sean, whose picture they very much wanted to see. The card, which contained a money order just for him, read (here unedited):

> We hope you and all your family are happy christmas, we are fine but can not to be forgetful, george, paula, meredith & sean. Very sorry because we don't see his face. Please send his picture to us.

Mrs. vongphet doesn't know will buy something for him—have money order (amount $30.00 inside this envelope.)

The card was signed by Kou, Vongphet, Kouvonsack, Vilalilach, Chanthasone, Souphaphone, and Vilavone, the youngest, then nine years old.

From time to time over the next several years, we exchanged greetings. But as things go we eventually lost touch. I'd like to think, and it is my hope, that they all are still well. I know my life, and my family's life, and the lives of sturdy Presbyterians living in a small midwestern town were changed by this remarkable family whose journey embodied the steadfast love of the God who makes all things new. I have wondered how I would have fared had I faced the ambiguity Kou faced. Would I, as he did, have kept going? Faced with such uncertainty, would I have had the tenacity to escape, the courage to cross a flooded river? Would I have boarded a plane and traveled halfway around the world, entrusting my life and my family to strangers living in a foreign land?

I know little about Kou's explicit faith. A cynic might conclude he is one more example of what desperate people do in desperate situations—they do what they must in order to survive. While I can't answer for Kou's explicit faith, he remains for me an example of what it looks like to walk in ambiguity while holding onto or being held by the steadfast love of the Lord, a love that gives pause to wonder, and wonder inspires resilience.

Perception is Not Reality

"What is" is framed by our point of view, but as the stories of Dietrich Bonhoeffer and the Homsombaths demonstrate, "what is" is not simply a matter of framing. War, resistance movements, despotism, dislocation, hunger, scarcity—in short, contingency itself—are not mere mental construals or fabrications. Perception shapes reality but reality is not merely perception. Moving trains arrive when they arrive, and the earth really moves.

Laying claim to the steadfast love of God does not allow us to paper over the human condition, or life at the boundaries, or even life at the center, but it does allow us to choose between despair and hope, between nihilism and what John's gospel calls "eternal life." Laying claim to God's steadfast love enables us to take hold of "what is" and to see it differently because "what is" is reframed by the larger truth of God's steadfast love.

In his 1942 Christmas letter, Bonhoeffer reflected on optimism. He observed that while pessimism allows us to avoid disappointment and ridicule, it is better to be optimistic. "The essence of optimism," he wrote, "is not its view of the present, but the fact that it is the inspiration of life and hope when others give in; it enables a man to hold his head high when everything seems to be going wrong; it gives him strength to sustain reverses and yet to claim the future."[11]

Bonhoeffer acknowledges in his letter that there is a "silly, cowardly kind of optimism," an optimism which must be condemned because it gives ultimate meaning to "chaos, disorder and catastrophe" or, alternately gives way to "resignation or pious escapism." He argues instead for optimism that accepts "responsibility for reconstruction and for future generations."[12]

In the closing, unfinished paragraph of that letter, which may have been written at the end of 1942 or perhaps the autumn of 1943, Bonhoeffer argues that we must "see the great events of world history from below, from the perspective of the outcasts, the suspects, the maltreated, the powerless, the oppressed, the reviled—in short, from the perspective of those who suffer."[13] This perspective, Bonhoeffer concluded, "must not become the particular possession of those who are eternally dissatisfied; rather, we must do justice to life in all its dimensions from a higher satisfaction, whose foundation is beyond any talk of 'from below' or 'from above.'"[14]

If we must have a point of view, and we must, it cannot be the basis or ground of our actions. Faith is not faith in a "perspective" or a "point of view," but rather the "higher satisfaction" of the Potter who spins the whirling earth, "calling into existence the things that do not exist" (Rom 4:17). The ground of our actions is the One who is making all things new, the One who asks, "I am about to do a new thing; now it springs forth, do you not perceive it?" (Isa 43:19).

For Reflection and Discussion

1. When or where have you observed and/or participated in ambiguity in ministry—in a nursing home where the one you prayed for had few if any options for significant change or health; in a board room when a major decision was about to be made; in relationships that are

---

11. Bonhoeffer, *Letters and Papers from Prison*, 15.
12. Ibid.
13. Ibid., 17.
14. Ibid.

routinely renegotiated; in your own heart when your back is against the wall?

2. How do you frame the past? Is the past simply past? How about the future? Is it simply "not yet"? How does your framing of the past and future diminish or enliven your passion for ministry?

3. In what ways have you experienced the newness of God's steadfast love? Consider your context for ministry. How have the people or institutions you have served experienced newness?

4. When was the last time you were surprised? What did you witness? What did you do? How did surprise affect the outcome of your actions?

5. What are some of the benefits of "a team of rivals"? What may be the dangers of "group think"?

6. Name a time when you ventured into "unknown unknowns." What did you do? How were you affected?

7. Bonhoeffer's poem, "Who Am I?," reflects a duality common to us all. How have you experienced this duality and what difference does God's steadfast love make in how you experience it?

8. When in ministry have you been compelled to surrender security? Name a time when you felt as if no ground was beneath your feet. How did uncertainty and your surrender to all security except the steadfast love of God change who you are and how you responded to your call?

CHAPTER SIX

Leading: It's About You

LIKE THE SIDES OF a single coin, this chapter and the next should be read in tandem. To lead we must follow and in following we are newly made—not destroyed, or absorbed, or obliterated—but newly made, freed, and sent to lead.

Leadership is both about and not about us. Leaders must show up, we must appear, and when we appear, we do so as witnesses, messengers, prophets, ambassadors, living sacrifices, servants, and ministers of Jesus Christ. We don't proclaim ourselves; we preach Christ crucified. We don't point to ourselves, but to the One who baptizes with the Holy Spirit and fire.

In this chapter, I want to explore the synergy between leading and following. We can't lead without first being led. And, to be led begins with identity: Who am I? Who am I in relationship to God in Jesus Christ? And how does that relationship shape my identity as a leader?

Who Are You?

In his 1921 book, *Psychological Types*, Carl Jung theorized that we experience the world through four principal psychological functions. Jung paired the four dichotomously—rational or judging functions, which he labeled *thinking* and *feeling*; and irrational, or perceiving functions, which he named *sensation* and *intuition*. Jung theorized that we typically have one strong suit, a "go-to" way of functioning. Some of us prefer thinking to feeling; some of us are more apt to interpret the world through sensations, others by intuitions.[1]

---

1. Jung, *Psychological Types*.

Prior to World War II, Katharine Cook Briggs and her daughter, Isabel Briggs Myers, considered Jung's typological theories and developed an inventory that aimed to identify personality preferences. The inventory was used to help women like Rosie the Riveter find the right fit as they entered the industrial work force. The inventory Katharine and Isabel developed was refined, field tested, and ultimately published in 1962 as the *Myers-Briggs Type Indicator*.

Using Jung's concepts, Briggs and Myers concluded that our preferences have multiple expressions. According to their theory, Jung's four types may be combined into sixteen expressions. In 1984, drawing upon Myers-Briggs and others, David Keirsey and Marilyn Bates, published *Please Understand Me: Character and Temperament Types*. I remember taking the self-administered inventory during a continuing education trip. I stayed up late one night to decipher my personality type. Was I an ESTP or an ESFJ? Was one better than another? I'm still not sure! It was a lot to keep up with. I wondered if I had answered the inventory honestly or had I only given answers that I thought I should give?

I'm certain that at some point in my life I've also taken the Myers-Briggs and once also the MMPI, or Minnesota Multiphasic Personality Inventory. As I recall, the MMPI was required screening as a part of my candidacy for ministry. I guess I must have passed, because they let me in!

I do not wish to make light of these and other inventories designed to help us figure out who we are. Personally, I found value in taking these tests and hearing the results from professionals. With each test, I learned something about who I am, what makes me tick, why I react the way I do or sometimes why I don't react as well as I should. I'm grateful for that self-awareness. Likewise, I think denominations are wise to use these and other inventories when discerning the aptitude and ability of leaders. We need all of the help we can get when it comes to sorting out who we are. I would only add this: discernment is a life-long process—becoming self-aware is life-long. It can't stop with one test or three, as if, once we get checked out and certified, we're home free. In fact, the more telling test or tests are the ones we face every day, year in and year out, whether we are making a hospital or nursing home visit or conducting a board meeting. In these moments, we must understand that leadership is "about us." And by that I don't mean that ministry is about us, as in, "look at me," but rather, absent self-awareness we are less able to be the leader God fashions us to be.

We get out of the way and let God be God when we know our place, our role, our limits. I am convinced that God is ever ready to let us know our limits, our role, our place, when we attend to the "voice speaking over the waters" (Ps 29:3). To say more about leadership and self-awareness, I want to explore Paul's notion about dying and rising in Christ and ask what that may mean for walking in wonder in ministry.

I No Longer Live?

As frequently observed, Paul's unusually brief salutation to the church at Galatia foreshadows things to come. Paul is not happy. He's "astonished" that his converts have so quickly deserted him and are turning to "a different gospel." Moments later he vents his spleen again when in effect he tells his opponents they can go to hell—"let them be accursed!" (Gal 1:9). The vitriol doesn't stop there. Paul accuses Peter not only of cowardice but hypocrisy (2:11ff). He names the Galatians "foolish" and wonders who "bewitched" them (3:1). Before the dust finally settles, Paul shouts that he wishes that those who are unsettling the Galatians "would castrate themselves" (5:12). Had Paul gone over the edge? Had he lost it? What was he so upset about? And "upset" hardly describes his mood.

For one thing, it seems Paul, as was his habit, doesn't like his authorization/credentialing called into question. He begins his letter there, from the first words that hit the papyrus: "Paul an apostle—sent neither by human commission nor from human authorities, but through Jesus Christ and God the Father" (1:1). He reiterates this claim three paragraphs later: "I want you to know, brothers and sisters, that the gospel that was proclaimed by me is not of human origin; for I did not receive it from a human source, nor was I taught it, but I received it through a revelation of Jesus Christ" (1:11–12).

With two thousand years of tradition and thousands of church buildings bearing Paul's name, Paul's claim has not lost its shocking arrogance. Imagine how it sounded to the Galatians. So, what was at stake? Just this: "If justification comes through the law [as Paul's opponents claimed], then Christ died for nothing" (Gal 2:21). At stake was the foundation of Christian faith: We are saved by Christ who died for the sins of the world and rose again. To drive home his counterclaim, Paul argues that through the law he died to the law so that he might live to God (Gal 2:19). He then makes this astounding claim: "I have been crucified with Christ; and it is no longer I who live, but it is Christ who lives in me" (Gal 2:20).

"I have been crucified with Christ; and *it is no longer I who live . . .*" (emphasis mine). Are we to think that Paul is actually dead, that what appears to be Paul is only a chimera, a phantom, a ghost? Are we to think that Paul is speaking metaphorically of his old self, that his former or shadow self has been crucified with Christ (Rom 6:6) and now a new self has emerged? What does Paul mean when he says "it is no longer I who live"? Does he mean his ego has died, his selfishness, his broken, distorted self—is that the "I" who no longer lives? And if that is the case, then who is the one naming Peter a coward and hypocrite? Who is the one telling the opposition to "go to hell"? Who is the one calling the Christians at Galatia "foolish" and "bewitched"? Who tells the opposition to "castrate themselves"? Was that Paul or Christ? Which "I" was speaking?

Paul tells us. We need not guess: "the life I now live in the flesh I live by faith in the Son of God, who loved me and gave himself for me" (Gal 2:20). Paul does not claim to be Christ. He is not a "little Christ." Paul is a new creation. He is God's work in progress. He still lives in "the flesh," which not only means that he is a living, breathing human being but one who is fully capable of spiteful name-calling and worse. Paul may long to "depart and be with Christ," but he is fully aware that it is not only better but necessary for him "to remain in the flesh" (Phil 2:23–24). Paul can exhort the Corinthians to imitate him as he imitates Christ (1 Cor 11:1), just as he can call upon his readers to see that the old has passed away and everything has become new—they are "a new creation" in Christ (2 Cor 5:17). But Paul never claims that he has become Christ. "We do not proclaim ourselves; we proclaim Jesus Christ as Lord and ourselves as your slaves for Jesus' sake" (2 Cor 5:5).

"*It is no longer I who live*, but it is Christ who lives in me." Christ alive in us does not absorb, or dissolve, or obliterate the self; rather, the self is transformed. A self cannot be transformed if it is undifferentiated from God, if it is somehow dissolved, or so completely absorbed that identity is lost. If we can become lost in God, one with God, why appeal, as Paul does in Romans 12, for the offering of our bodies to God as living sacrifices? If the "I" no longer lives, why "fight the good fight" or struggle "not to be conformed to this world"? If the "I" is dissolved, why then the need to be "transformed by the renewing of [our] minds, so that [we] may discern what is the will of God—what is good and acceptable and perfect" (Rom 12:2)?

The wonder of it all is that God does not overrule, or cast aside, or destroy the self but rather makes the self new. God delights in his creation. God delights in the girl now a young woman whose once sad eyes are now filled with the light of forgiveness. God rejoices in the boy now an old man who, once fearful, now proclaims good news without regard to his reputation, or honor, or safety, just as God rejoiced over one who once fiercely persecuted the church but is now known to us as St. Paul.

God works through us, through the uniquely gifted and sometime quirky and quarrelsome people we are. Grace does not erase identity but rather transforms it, making us into instruments of glory. To become those instruments, we must show up. That's why leadership is about us. To lead we must show up.

Before suggesting three ways transformed leaders rightly show up, I first want to sketch four ways leaders commonly "disappear." I then want to list five rules about how not to appear. Okay, I know that makes a total of twelve, which is eight more than Jung's four, but at least it's four less than Myers-Briggs' sixteen—I trust I'm not pushing my luck!

Four Ways We Disappear

Adam's phone rang at one a.m. When he entered the ER twenty minutes later, he quickly found David and Brooke, members of his church, surrounded by a clutch of sobbing high school seniors. The youth were friends of David and Brooke's seventeen-year-old son, Trent, who had just been pronounced dead. Word spread quickly through the small close-knit community. The deputy sheriff said Trent's Honda Civic was nearly torn in two when the eighteen-wheeler crossed the center line in a dense fog.

Adam crawled back into bed around four. Every bone in his body ached. His eyes stung from the tears he had shed. He had only one thought: "What will I say in two days when we bury Trent?"

In his 2011 book, Tom Long poses a question every minister must answer: "What shall we say?" What shall we say when we are the ones who must speak in the face of "evil, suffering, and the crisis of faith"?[2]

Most of us know what *not* to say—"I know what you're feeling." "This too shall pass." "Everything happens for a reason." "This was God's will." We are generally adept at knowing what *not* to say, but knowing what to say is another thing. Sometimes the silence is deafening.

---

2. Long, *What Shall We Say?*, title page.

Empathy and a ministry of presence take us only so far. Yes, we should know when to keep silence; we should know what *not* to say; but we must also *speak*. The gospel is not silent about the worst life hands us. Tragedy takes the wind out of us. And yes, it's tough finding the right words, but we cannot disappear in silence, not in the face of suffering nor in the presence of moral evil, which I will explore in the next chapter.

Pastoral speech, speech in the presence of suffering, requires empathy but also courage, courage grounded in hope. In 1977, Presbyterians adopted a confessional document titled *A Declaration of Faith*. The tenth chapter reads in part:

> Death often seems to prove that life is not worth living, that our best efforts and deepest affections go for nothing. We do not yet see the end of death. But Christ has been raised from the dead. . . . We are convinced the life God wills for each of us is stronger than the death that destroys us. . . . No life ends so tragically that its meaning and value are destroyed. Nothing, not even death, can separate us from the love of God in Jesus Christ our Lord.[3]

Pastoral speech, no less than prophetic speech, summons us beyond ourselves. Being fearful that we might say the wrong thing is no excuse for saying nothing.

"What shall we say?" Tom Long is right. Leaders must ask that crucial question, "What shall we say?" Pastoral speech, speech grounded in the cross and empty tomb, is one place to start; it is not the only place but maybe the first place to look for a beginning to our speech, not for answers to human suffering, but for testimony to the steadfast love of God in Jesus Christ.

In 1967, Thomas A. Harris, MD, published *I'm OK, You're OK*. By 1972, his book landed on the *New York Times* bestseller list and remained there for nearly two years. To date, over 15 million copies have been sold, making it one of the bestselling self-help books ever published.

Carl Rogers (1902–1987) was twice honored by the American Psychological Association for his research and contributions to psychotherapy, and was once nominated for a Noble Peace Prize for his work in Northern Ireland and South Africa. By many measures, Rogers ranks among the most eminent psychologists of the twentieth century. He is perhaps best known

---

3. Office of the General Assembly of the Presbyterian Church (U.S.A.), *A Declaration of Faith*, 23.

for his "non-directive" or "client-centered" theory of psychotherapy, later termed "person-centered" therapy.

I attended seminary from 1975 to 1978. Rogers and Harris were all the rage. Okay, I'll admit it—I thought they were great. Little did it occur to me that their assumptions flew in the face of my Calvinist heritage, disposition, and training. Why didn't it? I don't know. I suppose I was just as mystified or ensconced with the culture of narcissism as everybody else, my teachers included. I could not or did not see the disconnection between the humanism of Rogers and Harris and the theocentric humanism of Calvinism. For years, the disconnection allowed me to disappear when practicing ministries of pastoral care, counseling, and accountability.

Armed with Rogers and Harris, how could I ever offer a counter word to a church member, much less advice or wisdom? That was forbidden, or so I told myself. Best just to let folks work things out as they see fit; don't intervene or interfere; just make sure others come to their own conclusions, even if they are contrary to gospel demands. Hey, at least I was off the hook. I didn't have to call anyone into account. And then I started raising money. I'm kidding about that, but not really. I also began to question my "non-directive" pastoral methodology when I was forced to deal with absentee or nominal members, you know, Christmas and Easter Christians. Did I have any responsibility for them, to them? And if I did, what was it? Send a gentle reminder that the church was broke and would they please, please, pretty please send in a dollar? Or, gosh, actually call on members who hadn't darkened the door of the church for years, except for baptisms and weddings? Hey, I was off the hook. They knew best, right?

I'm being cheeky, but hardly so. Leaders cannot disappear when holding others accountable. We're not doing any favors by turning our back, satisfied with a "to each his own" approach. That's hardly the gospel. Likewise, we're hardly newly made leaders, or transformed leaders, or non-conforming leaders if we hide behind a cloak of anonymity when the boards we lead face tough decisions and we excuse ourselves from declaring where we stand. No, at times like these, we cannot disappear. We must show up. Before saying a word about how we do that or what that might look like, let me first identify what it doesn't look like—five wrong ways of showing up or appearing.

LEADING: IT'S ABOUT YOU

Five Rules for How *Not* to Appear, or Show Up

Rule number one: Don't bully or be a bully. I guess that should go without saying, but then again how many times have you been tempted like James and John to call down fire from heaven (Luke 9:51ff.) to consume those who threaten you?

Rule number two: When things get tough, don't scapegoat; don't find somebody in-house to blame. Yes, it will divert attention from you or whatever problems you and your congregation may be facing, but creating a scapegoat solves nothing. In fact, it diverts energy from where it needs to be, which is on the source of the problem, and which is also where solutions will be found.

Rule number three: Don't create external enemies; don't blame the national church for what's wrong with your congregation; don't blame "the government," or the "times we're living in," or liberal theologians, or conservative ones, or the fact that there simply aren't enough good Christians out there to join your church. It reminds me of a story a colleague told about a politician in a southern state who ran on a platform of prison reform. When he left office four years later, the press asked for an assessment. "Governor, how'd you do?" "Well, I'll tell you," the Governor began, "we tried, but I've come to this conclusion: this state needs better prisoners."

Rule number four: Don't play the *Who's a Better Christian* game. Remember the Corinthians? They had loads of fun playing *Who's a Better Christian?* Those Corinthians were clever. They had a party for everyone, even a Christ party, the Christian of all Christian parties. And guess what, everybody was miserable. Don't conquer by dividing. Nobody wins that game.

Rule number five: Don't get everybody focused on you. I know this chapter is titled, "Leading: It's About You," but we only lead as we are led and the last time I checked, we're not out front. There's one Leader, and it's not us. So, lead, as Ronald Heifetz advises, by giving the work back and by keeping the people you lead focused on their tough problems and not on you.[4] We lead by pointing to Christ, not to ourselves.

---

4. Heifetz, *Leadership Without Easy Answers*, 14–15.

Three Ways We Rightly Appear

I like being liked. I like people with bright eyes and big easy smiles. I like it when little old ladies ask for a hug. I like to hear old men talk about how it was back in their day. I like it when children run down the hall and hold out a drawing for me to keep that they made in Sunday school. I like to be liked. I appreciate being appreciated. I keep every thank you card in a bottom desk draw, along with letters expressing kindness, or encouragement, or how much it meant for me to "be there" when the need was great.

I like to be liked. I like helping people. It makes me feel good about being me when I help someone through a rough patch. I'm at my best when things around me couldn't be worse—a hospital ER, a contentious board meeting. I've never met a crisis I didn't like, not that I go looking for them. In thirty-five years, I've seen people go through and cause more tragic problems than I care to think about. I've also seen more wonderful things than I can count, more good things than bad. I try to remember the good; I try to forget the bad or give it to God when I have nowhere else to put it. That's all I know to do. Life is wonderful, but also complicated, difficult, tenuous. You name it; most pastors sooner or later will see it.

In part, we accept the challenges of ministry and muddle our way through because we like helping people and because most times we are generally able to draw upon a repertoire of relational skills that enable those we serve to get by, to survive, to flourish even. When things get tough, it's in our interest and in the interest of those we serve to be liked. If you're Adam and it's one a.m., it's nearly impossible to answer that call—assuming it's even made. If Trent's mom and dad think you're a jerk, or if they've had a "run in" with you that was never resolved, or if they are indifferent to you because you never made time to know them, then they won't call you.

Of course, pastors can be pastors to people they've never met, or hardly know, even to those who may dislike them, or whom they may dislike. I wouldn't argue that, but I would argue that one of the greatest traps of ministry is the need to be liked. We can trade off of it for only so long before it no longer works or before we've burned ourselves out by trying to please all the people all of the time. Ministry requires something better, something more enduring, something greater that will stand the test of time, and that is "speaking the truth in love" (Eph 4:15).

It is not coincidental that this beautiful phrase pops up in the thick of Paul's case for "making every effort to maintain the unity of the Spirit in the bond of peace." "There is one body," Paul says, "and one Spirit, just as you were called into the one hope of your calling, one Lord, one faith, one baptism, one God and Father of all, who is above all and through all and in all" (Eph 4: 4–5).

Paul is talking church. What holds it together? What grounds it? To be sure, its leaders: apostles, prophets, evangelists, pastors, teachers (Eph 4: 11). Leaders equip the saints, they build up the body until "all of us come to the unity of the faith and knowledge of the son of God, to maturity, to the measure of the full stature of Christ" (Eph 4: 12–13).

Paul understands that equipping and building and growing to "the full stature of Christ" do not happen in a vacuum; it's more likely a whirlwind. "We must no longer be children, tossed to and fro and blown about by every wind of doctrine, by people's trickery, by their craftiness in deceitful scheming" (Eph 4:14). To navigate storms, we need something more than being liked. Being liked or likeable won't cut it; rather, "speaking the truth in love, we must grow up in every way into him who is the head, into Christ from whom the whole body [is] joined and knit together..." (Eph 4:15).

Leaders best appear when they "speak the truth in love." And the truth is Christ. The truth is Christ holds the church together—not its leaders, not even its well-liked or beloved leaders. We lead best when we recover from the need to be liked and walk in the wonder of Christ who is the Head of his body. He is the joints and ligaments that enable "the body's growth in building itself up in love" (Eph 4:16). Don't worry about being liked, worry about "speaking the truth in love." That's the first way we rightly appear. The second is by speaking boldly (Phil 1:20).

Represent Christ, Speak Boldly

Ronald Heifetz observes that leadership has long been linked with authority or influence exerted by "Great Men" who are born with the right stuff, the right constitution and traits to make history. Other leaders, Heifetz notes, are made by history. They "rise to the occasion." Still other leaders, says Heifetz, are not only born but made. History shapes them and they shape history. Lastly, according to Heifetz, leaders emerge by a series of transactions by which they gain influence over their followers as well as adjust their leadership style to meet their followers' expectations.[5]

---

5. Ibid., 16–17.

Heifetz argues that leadership styles or theories about leadership are never "value free." "[T]heir values," he writes, "are simply hidden."[6] And not only "hidden" but in some instances "dangerous," as with, for example, the notion that "leaders are born and not made." That theory or assumption, Heifetz warns, "fosters both self-delusion and irresponsibility. [T]hose who consider themselves 'born leaders,' free of an orienting philosophy and strategy of leadership . . . [are] set-up for a rude awakening and for blindly doing damage." "Leadership," Heifetz concludes, "is more than influence."[7]

In his letter to the Philippians, Paul, writing from prison, asks for the Philippians' continued prayers, specifically that he "will not be put to shame in any way" (Phil 1:20). Paul hopes he will be released from prison but if not, even his death is gain. "It is my eager expectation and hope," Paul writes, "that I will not be put to shame in any way, but that by my speaking with all boldness, Christ will be exalted now as always in my body, whether by life or by death. For to me, living is Christ and dying is gain" (Phil 1:20–21).

Paul makes no apology for speaking boldly. Even in prison he is confident, but not because he is somehow mentally, or spiritually, or physically superior, or indifferent to his own suffering and possible death. Paul is bold; he speaks "with all boldness" because he is satisfied to be a witness. For him, that is enough. Paul is not on a pedestal. He leads by being led. He shows up because he's not the point, he's not the center. The focus is not Paul but Christ. "For me, living is Christ and dying is gain" (Phil 1:21). We are free to appear in ministry because we are not center stage. Like Adam, we can answer the late-night call because we represent Christ. We can show up because Christ shows up through us.

Don't Be Intimidated

I was afraid of my high school football coach. Actually, I was terrified of the man. And on some level, I suppose, I hated him. Rumor had it that he had been a Marine tank commander during the Korean War. I have no reason to doubt the truth of that. Coach wasn't a large man, but then as a six-foot-five-inch, 220-pound senior defensive end, not many seemed large to me. But with Coach size didn't matter. Words were his great weapon of

6. Ibid, 17.
7. Ibid, 20.

humiliation, and when that alone didn't work, he'd administer a slap to the helmet or a jerk of the face mask with "#$@&*" spitting from his mouth.

I suppose Coach's methods worked. We were good. Many of us had played together since middle school. In all of those years together, we had lost only a handful of games. By our senior year, there were high expectations. We did not disappoint. By the season's end we were undefeated and ranked number one in our state's highest division. We had broken every scoring and defensive record in our high school's history.

One Thursday, a game or two before the end of the regular season, Coach kicked me in the ass and yelled some obscenity at me because, as he said, "You're %#$* out of position." Thursdays were our "walk-through" day, when we reviewed Friday night's game plan in shorts and helmets. I was lined up defensively where Coach had drawn it up on the mimeographed sheet he'd handed out earlier in the day. He disagreed, so he kicked me and called me a "^%$*%" or something like that. When he turned his back to me I wheeled around and drew my fist back and would have knocked him to the ground had the line coach not grabbed me in a bear hug. Coach didn't say a word. He didn't have to. He never knew.

"Live your life in a manner worthy of the gospel of Christ," Paul urged the Philippians, "so that whether I come and see you or am absent and hear about you, I will know that you are standing firm in one spirit, striving side by side with one mind for the faith of the gospel, and are *in no way intimidated* by your opponents" (Phil 1:27–28; emphasis mine).

"Don't be intimidated." That's not a bad way to live, or to show up, or to appear when you lead. "Don't be intimidated." When we lead, it's not a question of "if" but "when" we will encounter resistance, opposition.

Churches, like human beings generally, are change averse, which is not to say that enabling change is the one or essential thing leaders do. Sometimes we do well to leave things alone. Change for the sake of change is foolish. But know this, when you lead you will meet opposition.

The greater question is what you will do when you meet opposition? For starters, don't be intimidated. And by that I don't mean be the toughest kid on the block; don't bully, or use intimidation in return, no, not at all. "If anyone strikes you on the right cheek, turn the other also" (Matt 5:39). The most powerful empire the world had ever known could not and did not intimidate Jesus. He was free. And so are those who follow him. Lead as you are led and you will lead others as Christ leads you. Don't be intimidated. Lead as Christ leads you.

For Reflection and Discussion

1. Think about your personality profile. What's your go-to function: thinking, feeling, sensing, intuiting? How does your profile influence your leadership style? Has your leadership style changed? If so, how?

2. Somewhere between Mr. Authority and Mr. Rogers there's a leader waiting to be expressed by you. What is your leadership style? Which leadership style best describes you? Can you name a time when you were so non-confrontational that you became ineffective? Likewise, can you name a time when you abused your authority? How do your expressions of authority shape your leadership?

3. Consider a time of pastoral crisis—perhaps like Adam in an ER. What did you do? Did you say too much? Too little?

4. Consider the relationship between being liked and "speaking the truth in love." Think about a pastoral care situation when you had to choose between the two. Think about a time when leading a board or institution you had to choose between the two. How did you choose? What were the consequences?

5. Bullying, scapegoating, blaming, dividing, or playing "holier-than-thou" card are some of the ways we divert attention from problem resolution or facing challenges. There are others. What would you name? What do you do to recognize these diversionary tactics and how can you stop them when you see them or employ them?

6. Do you ever find yourself trying to fix problems, either for a single person or for the entire parish? Over time, what happens when you are a "fixer"? What happens to you? What happens to the people you serve and/or work with?

7. Think about a time when you were intimidated. How do you respond to opposition, threat, resistance? How would your ministry be differently shaped if you were less intimidated?

CHAPTER SEVEN

Following: It's Not About You

Consider Your Call

MARTHA WAS FROM A prominent Charleston, South Carolina family. Was it five or six generations in Charleston? Martha could never quite remember and what's more she didn't care. Well, some days, she did. She enjoyed being noticed, being invited to the right parties, going to the right private school, but she was never like her brothers. They loved everything about Charleston. They fit right in. She envied their ease and charm. Like their father, they never met a stranger. They always had the right word and handsome good looks to boot. Martha avoided center stage, or tried to, anyway. But it was hard not to be noticed when you were a Middleton. Everybody knew who you were whether you knew them or wanted them to know you.

When it came time for college there was little discussion. Middletons went to Vanderbilt. And when they finished, they returned to Charleston. Middletons always came home. And that's just what Martha did. Her grades were better than average. Fact was she was bright, more than she let on. With a degree in finance and after a summer abroad, Martha came home, settled in a sea view cottage, and accepted the job offered to her at a locally owned bank. Her brothers, both older, were well into their careers and married with children. Other than marriage, not much had changed for them. They were happy as clams, flourishing. But not Martha.

Oh, Martha knew when and how to turn on her southern charm, but she was haunted by a deep awareness that there must be something more than the Charleston her brothers and family so loved. And it wasn't exactly

Charleston. It was Martha. And then late one afternoon over coffee with the associate pastor of her church, the pastor asked a question that changed everything. "Martha, have you ever thought about ministry?"

"Who? Me? You've got to be kidding. Whatever gave you that idea?"

"Oh, I don't know. You're always here. You never miss worship. You help with youth and you're a natural with older adults. Seems like a fit. It's just a hunch." Martha couldn't believe what she was hearing. Impossible. Incredible. "Who? Me?"

That day was eighteen years ago. For the last fifteen years, Martha has served small town congregations in rural Tennessee, which by most reckonings is a long way from Charleston, only now Martha is hauntingly at home.

"Consider your own call," Paul writes the Corinthians. "Not many of you were wise by human standards, not many were powerful, not many were of noble birth" (1 Cor 1:26). "Consider your own call . . ." What led you to ministry? What drew you? Like Martha, did it come as a surprise? What did you hear? How did you know? "Consider your own call."

In the previous chapter, I argued that ministers must be self-aware. We must know who we are. We must recognize our limits, our roles, our gifts, and consider how Christ transforms us when we walk in the wonder of his grace. Walking means we must show up. Disappearing is not an option. When we answer God's call to lead, Christ works through us for his purposes.

In this chapter, I want to accent following. Following is not about us. Following creates a new "us." Following creates freedom to lead, freedom to take risks, freedom to speak up and out. Following creates freedom to dream, to dare, to imagine. Following creates freedom to fail, freedom to start over, freedom to leave behind because we are captive to God's wondrous love in Jesus Christ.

Remember the call of Simon and Andrew "along the Sea of Galilee," where they were "casting a net?" It is so profoundly simple, "Follow me and I will make you fish for people. And immediately *they left their nets* and followed him" (Mark 1:18; emphasis mine). Simon and Andrew left their employment, the career they presumed they would pursue for as long as they lived, as most likely had their father before them. Likewise, consider James and John, who were "in their boat mending the nets." "Immediately [Jesus] called them; and *they left their father* Zebedee in the boat with the hired men, and followed him" (Mark 1:20; emphasis mine). Following is not about us. Following redefines not only who we are but what we do when we hear the "voice speaking over the waters" (Ps 29:3) and answer, "Speak, LORD, for your servant is listening" (1 Sam 3:9).

While I was writing this book, our congregation hosted a weekend for a guest lecturer and preacher. On Sunday night, in a crowded fellowship hall, I joined a table of eight with our guest speaker. I sat down next to a fifteen-year-old. He was eating mac and cheese and fried chicken. I introduced our guest speaker to the table and we soon enough broke into separate conversations. About halfway through dinner, the mother of the fifteen-year-old, seated across the table, piped up and asked me, "Has Harrison told you about one of his vocational options?"

"No."

"So," she says with a coy smile, "he's thinking about ministry!" I looked at Harrison, who had an equally playful smile. Raising his eyebrows, he nodded, "Yeah, we'll see."

That was it. No drama. No long, drawn-out conversation. I thought about asking Harrison if he wanted to talk, but decided against it. I asked his youth pastor if he'd mentioned anything to her about what he was thinking. "Nope, but then that's Harrison."

Where do "calls" come from? Harrison could be a Jeremiah or a Samuel—just a kid—and something is tugging on his soul, something is stirring in his heart. "Before I formed you in the womb I knew you, and before you were born I consecrated you; I appointed you a prophet to the nations" (Jer 1:5). Where does that come from?

When I consider my own call I can't readily explain it. I can tell you about growing up in a Christian home, going to Sunday school and church, youth group, participating in the Fellowship of Christian Athletes, and how there was a big gap between all of that and how I lived until I was a freshman in college and how my life began to change. I can tell you I joined briefly a group of charismatic Christians who spoke in tongues and who also believed that "mainline" seminaries were run by the devil. I can tell you I left that student-led group when they couldn't see my point about "fruits of the Spirit" being just as important as "gifts of the Spirit." I couldn't understand why they thought spectacular gifts were superior to moral fruits, so we parted ways. I can tell you that after my sophomore year I changed majors from business to religion and philosophy and was fortunate to find professors who introduced me to historical-critical biblical studies, church history, and theologians like Tillich, the Niebuhr brothers, Bonhoeffer,

Barth, and others. I can tell you that I had conversations with my pastor about ministry and that with his support and my church's help I went to seminary and accepted my first call when I was twenty-five years old. But I can't tell you during those years a precise moment when I heard God's call.

Like Martha, I never thought about being a minister. I didn't have a clue about what ministers did. Entering college I thought I might follow in my father's footsteps by majoring in business, or perhaps major in history or geology and coach high school football. Ministry was the last thing on my mind. But I was called. It's a mystery to me. And still is. Why me? I mean, I love what I do, most of it and most of the time, but I still find myself wondering, why me? Who am I to preach the word of God or to lead a people of God? How did that happen? It's not what I set out to do, but here I am. I can't say that it's been a cakewalk, a natural fit.

I sometimes feel as if I've lived a lover's quarrel with my chosen profession or the profession that's chosen me. I identify with Jeremiah when he complains, "O Lord you enticed me and I was enticed; you have overpowered me, and you have prevailed" (Jer 20:7). It's not every day nor every week, but every once in a while, I wish the call would go away. I sometimes wish I didn't have to speak or witness or lead, especially when "the word of the Lord" becomes "a reproach and derision" (Jer 20:8) or when "my close friends are watching for me to stumble" or are ready to take their revenge (Jer 20:10). And yet, and this is the part of calling that convinces me I am called: "If I say, 'I will not mention him, or speak any more in his name,' then within me there is something like a burning fire shut up in my bones; and I am weary with holding it in, and I cannot" (Jer 20:9). That for me is the wonder of wonders—that fire, the fire that makes me weary when I try to hold it in and cannot—fire I cannot control, or edit, or extinguish, fire that keeps me walking when I'd rather sit down and rest, or disappear, going gently into the night.

We each have a call to tell. However told, calling reminds us that ministry is not about us. Leading is about following the Crucified and Risen Lord. Leading is not about showing off our talents or even "being used" as if God needed us. Leading is about surrendering our will to God's will in our particular time and circumstance. H. Richard Niebuhr named this surrender "the enduring problem" of Christian faith.[1] What shape does faith take in the "real world," not just individually but collectively? How shall we live? How shall we give a faithful witness at the crossroads of reason and

---

1. Niebuhr, *Christ and Culture*.

revelation, religion and science, natural and divine law, state and church, nonresistance and coercion?[2]

Niebuhr identified five types or answers classically given to that question. According to Niebuhr, while God is absolute, how faith takes shape in the world is relative, fluid, changing. The way or ways we respond to God's call vary. It would be a mistake to freeze frame one response and claim it is the right response for all time.

Niebuhr's types should be seen as patterns of behavior or perhaps constellations of theological claims. He does not imagine that we are always locked into one type. Over time we may adopt aspects of each type or several at once. Looking through the lens of Niebuhr's typology, I want to explore five modes of following or answering God's call, while observing why leading is not about us. I will begin where Niebuhr does: "Christ Against Culture," and follow his sequence throughout: "Christ of Culture," "Christ Above Culture," "Christ and Culture in Paradox," and "Christ the Transformer of Culture."

"Christ Against Culture"

On Christ the King Sunday, 2002, three months before the US invasion of Iraq, I preached a sermon titled "Oil, Terror, and the Power of Hope." My texts were Ezekiel 34:1–13 and Ephesians 1:15–22. Two weeks later I sat in a law office across the table from two families in my church who wanted me to keep my mouth shut about politics. They read a formal letter of complaint, citing quotes from my sermon, which they deemed "political." They didn't want my job; they wanted me to stay out of politics in the pulpit.

I can't say that I blame them for their complaint. I've listened to sermons that I thought were "political." Where do we draw the line? What constitutes a "political" sermon? In 1979, I preached a sermon during the SALT II negotiations. Afterward, one member angrily asked if I would preach the same sermon after Russian tanks had rolled down Main Street and soldiers had raped my wife. "How would you think about disarmament then?" she bitterly asked.

In March 1981, near the first anniversary of the assassination of Archbishop Oscar Romero, I preached a sermon about US involvement in El Salvador. While I was greeting the congregation afterward, a young woman,

2. Ibid, 10.

about my age, asked for "equal time" in the pulpit next week. "There are two sides to every issue," she said. And she was right.

Whenever I've preached on hot button issues, I've wondered if the complaints might have been compliments had I taken the complainers' side. What if I had backed the war in Iraq? What if I had applauded the contras in El Salvador? What if I had said, "Hell no, we're not disarming our nukes." Would the complainers have complained? Would they have thought I was speaking "politically"? Or might they have complimented my bold stand for right?

"Do not love the world or the things in the world. The love of the Father is not in those who love the world . . ." (1 John 2:15). Seen through the lens of First John, sermons concerning foreign policy might be named "worldly" and hence irrelevant. "What business is it of ours to be worried about US foreign policy? Stick to the gospel." Funny thing is, when I preached those sermons named above, I thought I was "sticking to the gospel." I thought I was championing the Prince of Peace, the God of justice. I thought I was preaching the gospel. I could do no other. Silence wasn't an option. The Lordship of Christ trumped silence and what I deemed cultural accommodation, a gospel domesticated, conformed to the world.

Leading is not about us when following Christ demands we take unpopular stands and the stands may fall politically and socially or morally and theologically to the right or left. It doesn't matter. Opposition may come from either side. Following Christ can't be a popularity contest. When called, sometimes we are protest leaders, crusaders, campaigners, champions, prophets. Jesus put it this way, "Woe to you when all speak well of you, for that is what their ancestors did to the false prophets" (Luke 6:26).

Leadership is not about pleasing people; it's about leading or following Christ no matter where that may take us. We're not the point but on occasion we must take the point. When you do, do as a friend once told me; "leave room for others to stand."

"Christ of Culture"

I have a confession to make. It's a little late in coming—thirty years, give or take—but I was the one who kept removing the American flag from the sanctuary without asking or telling anyone about it. I'm guilty. When no one was around, I hid the flag in the sanctuary storeroom. A few weeks, maybe a month would go by and somebody would notice the flag missing

FOLLOWING: IT'S NOT ABOUT YOU

and they'd return it to its station at the front of the sanctuary. A week, maybe two later, I would hide it again.

So, why did I remove the flag? Well, I had the idea that the church of Jesus Christ ought to be the church of all people and not just Americans. I had the idea that the flag represented a domesticated, watered down, worldly, culturally accommodated Protestantism. I had the idea that the flag put nation and God on par with each other or rather that God was in service to the nation.

I've also felt that way when I've prayed before high school football games or chamber of commerce events or city and county council meetings. I've felt that way, and kicked myself for it, when I've preached sermons that were reasonable when the text for the day was nothing short of outrageous. I've felt that way when I've used psychotherapy rather than prayer or when I've substituted hard-headed stubbornness for something called hope. I've felt that way when I was a manager or administrator of an institution rather than a priest or pastor or prophet of the people of God. In short, I have betrayed the gospel when I have enjoyed too cozy a relationship with the water or culture in which I swim.

When we serve the Christ of Culture we really don't need Christ—culture will do. Creation is basically good, and redemption, if there is such a thing, only improves it. After all, we are one big happy family—the fatherhood of God and the brotherhood of man—you know, Rodney King's "Come on people, let's get along." I don't know if Rodney said it just that way, but you get my point. "Come, let us reason together. Let's talk." I believe in talking and I also believe in reason, but talking reasonably doesn't lead us to the kingdom of God.

Yes, I'm aware that Paul said that we all should be "subject to the governing authorities" and that "there is no authority except from God . . . the authority does not bear the sword in vain! It is the servant of God . . ." (Rom 13:1ff.). Yes, I'm aware that Jesus said that he came not to "abolish the law or the prophets . . . but to fulfill" (Matt 5:17). I am also aware that he said we should "Give therefore to the emperor the things that are the emperor's . . ." (Matt 22: 21). But I am just as aware that Jesus never specified what we owe the emperor. Likewise, Paul might have had a different take on authority had he not thought the "night" so "far gone" or "the day" so "near" (Rom 13:11–12). Had Paul lived to see and write about Nero, he might have written more like John of Patmos, who compared the authority of Rome to the "dragon . . . a beast rising out of the sea" (Rev 13:1).

So, what am I saying? Just this: when Christ is "of" culture, we can manage, live, exist, thrive, etc. just as well without Christ. Who needs Christ when all you really need is self-reliance, more esteem, or a new and improved social safety net, or a more just state? Christ might be a prime example, an idea of "the good" or "the true," but Christ is hardly needed for a world we create and manage. And if we don't need Christ, what use are ministers of Christ? If Christ is "of" culture then we actually can disappear for then we have no one to follow except ourselves or the crowd in front of us.

"Christ Above Culture"

"Hey George; good morning. You got a minute?"

"Sure, what's up."

"We're having a meeting here at First Church next week and I thought it might interest you. We're thinking about creating a hospice. Have you heard about hospice?"

"A little, not much."

"In a nutshell, hospice tries to care for the dying and their families. Many choose to die at home; some, because their symptoms can't be managed, choose the hospital, but we stay with them until the end. We also provide grief counseling and support afterward."

"Who's the *we*? Who provides this help?"

"Volunteers, people like you. Are you interested?"

"Yeah, I'll be there. Sounds like a good thing. I'm interested."

"Then we'll see you Tuesday."

"Deal."

We started small: one part-time nurse-manager and twenty-five or so volunteers. Aside from the nurse-manager, caregivers were volunteers; all services were free of charge. Eventually, insurers and Medicare recognized hospice and began reimbursements, so we incorporated. The pastor of First Church was elected president; I was elected vice-president. He was good at raising money; I was good at managing it. After four years, we dedicated the first free-standing in-patient hospice in our state. Our professional staff numbered twenty; volunteers were in the hundreds. Most important of all, the love of God was expressed in countless ways to the dying and their families.

FOLLOWING: IT'S NOT ABOUT YOU

During my sophomore year in college and some months after I had "gotten religion," I was home for fall break or Christmas, I can't remember which. But I do remember a conversation I had with my father, or the gist of it. "The institutional church is dead," I said sharply and smugly. "It's full of hypocrites and those who do go don't half-believe what they say they believe. I'm leaving the church."

"But, son, look at all of the good the church has done throughout history—all of the hospitals and schools it's built, aid given to faraway places, changes made in labor laws, government even."

"Maybe, but I think God is judging the church, going outside the church. I want to do street ministry. You know, I want to go where real people are, those who know they need help. The people at our church don't need anybody's help, least of all Jesus.'"

I was a smartass and wrong. Of course I couldn't or didn't see it then. My new religion had produced a different sort of hypocrite, one who looked down on institutions, the establishment. I was a member of the "pure" church; first-century Christianity was my religion.

My father's religion, like his politics, was that of the middle. Niebuhr named this church the "Church of the Center" or the "synthetic" church—the church that is not against culture or of culture but "above" it. The "Church of the Center" puts Christ and culture together.

For the greater part of my ministry, I have led the "Church of the Center," which is ironic given my youthful aspirations. The "Church of the Center" is full of nice people who like to do nice things for others. And that's not a bad thing. The "Church of the Center" is full of reasonable people. Okay, I'll grant the outliers—those extremists who take religion too seriously, those who stir up trouble with big ideas about changing the world for Christ, winning the world for Christ, those who desire a purer form of Christianity, one less tainted by the world.

By contrast, progressives and their moderate cousins are more realistic. They know that change takes time; Rome wasn't built in a day. And since moderates and progressives are generally financially comfortable, they can afford to wait. They can afford the luxury of time. They aren't driven by apocalyptic energy and urgency. They have all the time in the world to wait and to put things together, to bring together ideas and resources to make the world a better place. My father was right about that. For all of the knocks against it, and there are many, the "Church of the Center" has done a world of good. It has educated masses, passed legislation to end oppression. The

"Church of the Center" has helped create a social foundation to support an environment that favors human flourishing. That is its great achievement and also its greatest weakness.

The "Church of the Center" is always in danger of sliding comfortably into human achievement while shutting its eyes to radical evil and an even more radical grace. Leaders of the "Church of the Center" ignore this tendency at their own peril and at the peril of the church they love. Jesus didn't come to make us nice; he came to redeem creation.

"Christ and Culture in Paradox"

Ernie was a great kid with a million dollar smile. Though he was not exactly a saint or model citizen, you couldn't help but like him. His mischief was not harmful. Hurt wasn't in him, but mischief most likely contributed to his death when the car he was driving flipped off a mountain road. Ernie was twenty-one.

What do you say to Ernie's parents, or to his friends, or to the congregation that took vows at his baptism and watched him grow up?

What do you say to the father of the twenty-five-year-old who shot himself one night in a drunken stupor? What do you say to first-time parents whose child was born dead? What do you say to the mother of a sixteen-year-old girl who was raped and then murdered? What do you say to the fifty-two-year-old who lost his job and is about to lose his home because he can't find work? What do you say to the forty-two-year-old who just learned she has an inoperable brain tumor and has less than six months to live? What do you say to Joey, who returned from Afghanistan without his legs? What do you tell yourself about the plight of "the bottom billion," while you diet to stay in clothes you don't need?[3]

"My kingdom is not from this world. If my kingdom were from this world, my followers would be fighting to keep me from being handed over . . ." (John 18:36).

"[T]he appointed time has grown short; from now on, let even those who have wives be as though they had none, and those who mourn as though they were not mourning, and those who rejoice as though they were not rejoicing, and those who buy as though they had no possessions and those who deal with the world as though they had no dealings with it. For the present form of this world is passing away" (1 Cor 7: 29–31).

3. Collier, *The Bottom Billion*.

This reality, the world we inhabit, is not final reality. Bonhoeffer called it penultimate or next to the last. Bonhoeffer's tradition resolved the tension between penultimate and ultimate reality with Luther's "two kingdoms." Christ is not of, or against, or above culture, but in some sense "between" time and eternity, which means that his followers are strangers to this world, sojourners, wandering pilgrims who are never completely at home.

Followers of this Christ live with two-ness, duality, in but not of the world, holding but never fully owning; not indifferent, above, or aloof from the world, but not fully at home. So we endure, we wait, we fight the good fight until the day of new creation, deliverance that never completely touches or fully transforms this life. Therefore we wait with hope. In this world, the only God who helps is the God who suffers—the crucified God.

I don't think we try to explain that. Leaders who follow the crucified God can't explain radical evil. To do so would give it too much power, legitimacy. No, instead, followers of the crucified cry out in protest against evil. Death remains the last enemy and whatever gains we have, we count as loss (Phil 3:7). Leaders following the crucified God take themselves lightly, realizing that whatever they build is passing away. Leaders of the crucified God do not rely on their gifts or talents or savvy. They have no ground to stand on except the cross and the radical grace that saves them. They are not in charge; they are witnesses. They are not professionals; they proclaim good news in a sometimes dark and tragic world. The form of this world is passing away. Hold it lightly.

"Christ the Transformer of Culture"

The church I lead serves 1,000 meals a week to the urban poor. Some of our guests are homeless, some are transients, some are mentally ill, some are addicts, some are the working poor. On Monday mornings, before breakfast, our choir director leads a seven o'clock gospel sing-a-long for guests who choose to join in. On Tuesdays and Thursdays, Bible studies are led by lay leaders and a seminary intern. Generally, once a month, communion is served. When funding is sufficient flu shots are given. At Christmas, we have a big party with gifts.

Are we changing the world by this ministry? Are we addressing systemic conditions that foster poverty? Are we solving "the hunger problem" or "the homeless problem"? Not completely. We're doing our best to hold creation and redemption together. Creation is distorted, warped, misdirected.[4] Creation, however flawed and broken, is nonetheless the theater of God's glory. We suffer no illusions. We try to love our neighbors and welcome them as Christ has welcomed us, and by doing so the world, however briefly, or fragmentally, or partially, is changed.

"Do not be conformed to this world, but be transformed by the renewing of your minds, so that you may discern what is the will of God—what is good and acceptable and perfect" (Rom 12:2).

"Be transformed." Transformation is not something we do to ourselves. Transformation is something that happens to us. This is what wonder is about. We are changed by the mercy of God, mercy that enables us to surrender our lives "as a living sacrifice" (Rom 12:1). That's the point of God's mercy—restoring what is lost, bringing together what has been torn apart, reshaping the distorted, delivering us from evil and clothing us again in our right mind (Mark 5:15). That's not our work; that's God's work. We are midwives to it. And God's mercy is new every morning!

Leaders who follow this Christ don't create the baby but they do help bring it into the world. We don't see fully how the baby will turn out; we see dimly and that is enough. Following the One who transforms creation and who brings it to completion doesn't let us off the hook, but it does make the burden lighter. We're not the point; we point to the One who is—Jesus Christ crucified and risen from the dead.

For Reflection and Discussion

1. "Consider your own call . . ." What led you to ministry? What drew you? What did you hear? How did you know? How has your call shaped your ministry?

2. Have you ever wished you hadn't accepted your call? If so, why?

3. Have you ever taken an unpopular stand on a moral or social or political issue and found yourself in "hot water"? If so, what did you go through? Did you make enemies, lose church members, or perhaps make new friends or gain a new perspective from those who opposed you?

4. Using a scale of one to five, with five being high, rate your need to please people. How has "people-pleasing" factored into your ministry?

4. Niebuhr, *Christ and Culture*, 194.

5. What risks or dangers have you observed when the church is too closely aligned with culture?

6. What's wrong with being nice? Aren't Christians supposed to be nice? Do you ever get tired of leading a church of nice people? If so, why?

7. Ministers deal with tough, sometimes tragic issues. How do you deal with tragedy? How do you deal with the gaps between what is and the kingdom of God?

8. When have you been "a midwife" to the transformation of the world? What did you do? What did you experience? What changed? How were you changed? How was your church changed? How did the world change?

CHAPTER EIGHT

Resilience: A Christ-Shaped Life of Freedom

Profiles in Resilience

JOHN RAE (1813–1893) GRADUATED from Edinburg University with a degree in medicine and soon went to work for the Hudson Bay Company. He was posted to Moose Factory, Ontario, population 180. He spent his first Christmas there in 1834.

Rae was a wanderer. He also possessed extraordinary stamina and an equally deep curiosity that led him to embrace Inuit culture and learn from it. By 1846, Rae struck out on the first of four major explorations he led. Over eight years Rae travelled more than 23,000 miles—6,504 in the Arctic alone, mostly on snowshoes, and another 6,634 miles in canoes and small boats. Before retiring to London, Rae would discover the fate of fellow explorer Sir John Franklin, while mapping the final link in the Northwest Passage.[1]

Diana Nyad (1949-present) was born in New York City. After her parents' divorce and her mother's remarriage, the family moved to Fort Lauderdale, Florida, where as a middle school student Diana began swimming competitively. Her efforts were rewarded with state championships in the backstroke at 100 and 200 yards. In 1966 Diana suffered a three-month long heart infection. When she returned to the pool, her speed was diminished, dimming whatever aspirations she entertained for the '68 Olympics. It was then that Diana turned to marathon swimming. By 1970 she gained

---

1. McGoogan, *Fatal Passage*, 304–5.

international recognition, setting a women's world record in a ten-mile swim in Lake Ontario.

Nyad is perhaps best known for her 2013 swim from Havana, Cuba to Key West, Florida, completed at the age of sixty-three. Between August 31 and September 2, she covered a distance of nearly 110 miles. Diana was in the water for fifty-three hours. It was her fifth try. Her first four attempts were foiled by everything from rough seas to asthma, from unfavorable currents to Portuguese man-of-war stings.

Ernest Shackleton (1874–1922) was preparing to cross Antarctica via the pole when his expedition ship, *Endurance*, became trapped in pack ice. The date was January 19, 1915. Realizing that he would have to wait until the September spring thaw, Shackleton ordered the ship abandoned. September came and went. Toward the end of October, under extreme pressure from sea ice, the *Endurance* began taking on water. One month later it slipped beneath the icy sea. The ship's slow death allowed the twenty-eight-member crew to salvage provisions for the coming winter while camped on a large, flat floe. By March the expedition had journeyed to within sixty miles of land, but separated by impassable ice. Shackleton ordered the crew into three salvaged lifeboats. After five days in stormy seas, the men landed on Elephant Island, 346 miles from where the *Endurance* met its fate.

Help was a long way off, 800 miles to be exact. Whaler stations on South Georgia, Island were the only hope. Choosing five companions for the journey and provisions for no more than four weeks, Shackleton boarded the *James Caird*, a twenty-foot refitted open lifeboat, setting sail on April 24, 1916. Sixteen days later, after enduring hurricane force winds, the crew landed on South Georgia's southern shore. Help was still thirty-two miles away—on the north shore where the whalers were stationed. Fearing stormy seas and a rocky coastline, Shackleton and two other companions attempted a land crossing over the mountainous terrain. Thirty-six hours later they arrived at the whaling station at Stromness. Three months later, after three failed attempts due to deadly sea ice, Shackleton, with help from the Chilean government, reached his crew on Elephant Island. Not a single soul was lost. All twenty-two survived.[2]

John Rae, Diana Nyad, and Ernest Shackleton are extraordinary examples of human resilience. Their capacity to bounce back from prolonged and profound distress is nothing short of astonishing. The capacity to "bounce back" is at the heart of resiliency. We are resilient when we "spring

---

2. Shackleton, *South*.

back" or "rebound." Physics recognizes resiliency as physical energy stored in an elastic material when it is deformed. Think of a rubber ball. When compressed and released it resumes its original form. Likewise, ecology understands resiliency as an ecosystem's capacity to return to its original state after being disturbed. Think of a forest after a fire or a river after a flood.

Of course you don't have to be an arctic explorer or open water endurance swimmer to display resiliency. Think about the people you know who care for aging parents with dementia, or single parents raising a family while working full-time, or the unemployed who stand in long lines on the off chance that they might find a job, even work for which they are overqualified. Think about workers who wake up every morning only to return to jobs they don't like. Think about young adults whose hearts are broken when the breakup happens that ends their dream for marriage, or the recently widowed who feel as if life can't possibly go on, or the newly retired whose golden years are more rust than gold.

Resiliency is necessary to life; in fact, resiliency is built into life. It is a gift of God's creative energy, animating all things and in some instances reanimating them. I want to make a case for resiliency not only as a gift of creation, naturally occurring, but also a gift of grace, a gift given by the Redeemer, the Enchanter, Jesus Christ.

Get Up

"The person who is wakened," writes Jürgen Moltmann, "has to get up. Unless he does, the waking is ineffective."[3] Wonder is a form of wakefulness; it is an awakening from our sleep to God's wonders, not a steady state or posture, but a response to the God "who gives life to the dead and calls into existence the things that do not exist" (Rom 4:17). When we hear "the voice over the waters" we "get up" and get going. We bounce back and attend once more to the One who calls. We are not our own. Of course we don't always live believing that. We sleep. We are "buffered" and sometimes disenchanted. We can't hear the Voice, so we sleep either in acedia or hubris. Still, the Voice calls to us over the waters, crying, shouting out, "Get Up!"

Luke tells us that Jesus met ten lepers in a village "between Samaria and Galilee," a kind of no-man's land. The lepers approached Jesus, though cautiously, crying out, "Master have mercy on us" (Luke 17:13). Following Jewish custom, Jesus ordered the ten to go and show themselves to the

3. Moltmann, *The Way of Jesus Christ*, 247.

priests. On their way, they were healed. One, a Samaritan, returned and fell at the feet of Jesus praising God. Jesus wondered about the nine, "Where are they? Was none of them found to return and praise God except this foreigner" (Luke 17:18)? No answer is given, not a word. The episode ends with a pronouncement, a command to the foreigner at the feet of Jesus, "*Get up* and go on your way; your faith has made you well" (Luke 17:19; emphasis mine).

"Get up and go on your way." It is a command, but also an invitation. Wonder does not leave us "lost" but redirects, stands us up, sending us on our way. Our tendency is to sleep, our tendency is to wander, not wonder. Nowhere is that more evident than in Gethsemane, the garden of suffering, the garden of decision.

According to Mark, Jesus took Peter, James, and John with him to Gethsemane. Jesus is "distressed and deeply agitated." Jesus wants company but also space: "I am deeply grieved, even to death; remain here, and *keep awake*" (Mark 14:34; emphasis mine). Parting from them, Jesus walks more deeply into the night. Throwing himself on the ground, he prays that "the hour might pass from him." Acknowledging that "all things are possible," he prays for the cup to be removed. Jesus doesn't want to die, but ends his prayer: "yet, not what I want but what you want" (Mark 14:36). A decision has been reached, or almost. Jesus returns to the disciples and finds them sleeping. "Could you not *keep awake* one hour? *Keep awake* and pray that you may not come into the time of trial; the spirit is indeed willing but the flesh is weak" (Mark 14:38; emphasis mine).

Once again Jesus leaves the disciples. Mark says "he went away and prayed, saying the same words"—"let this hour pass, remove this cup, all things are possible, nevertheless, not my will." A second time Jesus returns to the disciples; again they are "sleeping, for their eyes were very heavy; and they did not know what to say to him" (Mark 14:40). Have the disciples had too much wine? Is the hour late? Perhaps both, but Mark's greater emphasis is that the Messiah stays awake and wrestles with God while the disciples sleep, not because they've had too much to drink or because it's late, but rather because this hour is God's hour and God alone faces it for his sleeping disciples. Mark reiterates the solitude of this hour when Jesus leaves the disciples sleeping a third time and upon his return announces, "Are you *still sleeping* and taking your rest? Enough! The hour has come . . . *get up*, let us be going" (Mark 14:41; emphasis mine). "The hour" will change everything—the disciples will rise from sleeping to waking. They will get up and get going.

Sleeping, like Taylor's term "buffering," is an apt metaphor for disenchantment or perhaps better, arrested enchantment. When asleep, we don't expect much. With eyes wide shut, we cannot see or expect to see. So is there anything we can or should do? Yes. Get up! And we can "get up" because One has risen before us, the "first fruits of those who have died" or "fallen asleep" as the Greek word literally reads (1 Cor 15:20).

"*Sleeper, awake*! Rise from the dead, and Christ will shine on you" (Eph 5:14; emphasis mine). We answer the command to "get up" by wakefulness, alertness, readiness, anticipation, and—most importantly of all—walking, following. Resiliency is formed by a life of response to the One who does not sleep, to the One calling us to awaken. We bounce back when we are pulled, drawn, raised up. God does wonders and we wake up to wonder. God wakes us up and we are amazed, astonished, puzzled, perplexed, awed; we are made alive, awake to the One in our midst. Resilience is exodus from slavery to acedia and hubris; resilience is resurrection from sin and death. In short, resilience expresses a Christ-shaped life of freedom.

Exodus and Resurrection, Freedom of New Creation

God is not indifferent to the human condition nor to creation itself. God longs to wake up creation and each of us. "Let there be light" (Gen 1:3). It is worth noting that Paul locates human longing for redemption within the longing of creation itself. Creation "groans"; it waits with eager longing (Rom 8:19). It is not simply that creation is a place where human redemption occurs, a kind of disposable stage. No, "creation itself will be set free from its bondage to decay . . ." (Rom 8:18). Or, as the seer put it, "I saw a new heaven and a new earth; for the first heaven and the first earth had passed away, and the sea was no more" (Rev 21:1).

When Paul considered creation and redemption he counterposed "freedom" with "futility." The Greek word for futility may be alternately translated *emptiness, purposelessness, frustration, uselessness, worthlessness, idleness, transitoriness*. Creation is not as it should be nor is it as it shall be. God is not indifferent to the human condition or to creation itself. God hears. God takes notice: "Out of the slavery their cry for help rose up to God. God heard their groaning. . . . God took notice of them" (Exod 2:23).

When God takes notice, when God hears, he "remembers." And when God remembers, God acts; he sends, he "comes down to deliver" (Exod 3:8). God brings freedom, freedom from futility, freedom from bondage to decay, until all things, until the whole of God's creation, shall "obtain the freedom of the glory of the children of God" (Rom 8:21).

Exodus and resurrection lead to freedom and new creation. Paul suggests that we are newly created and experience freedom when "we cry, 'Abba, Father!'" That prayer, the cry of Jesus in dark Gethsemane, is testimony from the Spirit of God "bearing witness with our spirit that we are children of God" (Rom 8:15–16). Exodus and resurrection are not acts of self-help or discovery. Paul's metaphor in Romans 8 is "adoption." Through the testimony of the Spirit, we become what we are not—"children of God, and if children, then heirs, heirs of God and joint heirs with Christ" (Rom 8:17). When we "wake up" from our sleep we become children of God. Awakening, wonder, and enchantment lead to new identity in Christ. We are redeemed and brought to new life.

Paul does add a provision to new creation, a condition, not a transaction, but a requirement, a summons, the command of the Crucified and Risen One—"Follow me." Or, as Paul reiterates, "if, in fact, we suffer with him so that we may also be glorified with him" (Rom 8:17).

Suffering with and for the Crucified moves us away from a life curved in on itself. Suffering moves us toward the neighbor. "Whoever says, 'I abide in him,' ought to walk just as he walked" (1 John 2:6). Jesus walked with and for the neighbor, for his brothers and sisters. Freedom given in new creation is not freedom from others but freedom for others. This horizon of redemption, as described by Jürgen Moltmann, is not simply individual or social but generational and cosmic.[4] Jesus doesn't die simply *for me* or *for us* but for all generations, indeed, for creation itself.

Resilient ministry abides in a broad frame. Too often we limit our frame of reference. We provide pastoral care to one person at a time. Likewise, we run like mad to keep up with "the church" or "our congregation." We tend the "flock." We run to keep it together, growing, flourishing, faithful. And we should. Ministers are obligated to attend to individual and community needs. That's our job. Yet, we must also work from a broader frame, one that considers generations that come after us and those that have gone before us, the broader frame of the whole created order.

---

4. Ibid., throughout.

Jesus is not just *my* Lord and Savior or even *our* Lord and Savior. He is, as Paul expressed it, "the first born of all creation; for in him *all things* in heaven and on earth were created, things visible and invisible, whether thrones or dominions or rulers or powers—*all things* have been created through him and for him. He himself is before *all things*, and in him *all things* hold together" (Col 1:15–17; emphasis mine). This broader frame provokes, inspires, indeed requires, nothing less than walking in wonder.

It's a big world. And a big world creates and calls for a wonder-filled faith. The psalmist expressed it this way: "One generation shall laud your works to another, and shall declare your mighty acts. On the glorious splendor of your majesty, and on your wondrous works, I will meditate" (Ps 145:4–5). Walk in that frame (in Christ, with Christ) and you will be awed by the mystery of God. You will be free. You will be newly created and made resilient for the journey. To explore possible trajectories of this journey, I want to consider three offices held by ministers, classically expressed as prophet, priest, and pastor. There are other roles we play, but these three are essential. My aim is to illustrate some examples of resilient ministry in Christ-shaped freedom.

Prophet

The cursor on Hannah's computer monitor mocked her: "Blink? Blink? Blink? What are you going to write today, Hannah? It's 7 a.m., Thursday, you know—sermon writing day—and it's stewardship season, again. What do you have? Blink? Blink? Blink?"

Hannah retraced her steps over the last month: one funeral; multiple hospital visits with a fifty-six-year-old in the throes of chemotherapy; nursing homes visits with seniors; a late afternoon conference with a thirty-two-year-old facing divorce. Hannah tried collecting her thoughts. "God is good. God is generous."

"No. That won't do," Hannah grimaced. She stabbed *Delete*.

Hannah's thoughts drifted forward to the father of three who was laid off after seventeen years with the same company. "How am I going to preach to him about stewardship? And what about Susan, a single mom with two kids, an office secretary? And then there's Harriet and Will with nothing but Social Security and little of that. How can I preach about money when so many are struggling just to make ends meet?"

Hannah tried again, "God is generous. God is good." Once again she hit *Delete*. "Ugh," she sighed, "I just don't have it today. What am I going to say? The stewardship packets are already in the mail. We've just finished six weeks of budget planning. Is that all down the drain because I can't find the right words, God's Word?"

Hannah got up. She paced. She thumbed through several books. She felt like crying and then it hit her; it came to her, a dim memory from Paul. It struck her with quickening light: "God is able to provide you with every blessing in abundance, so that by always having enough of everything, you may share abundantly in every good work" (1 Cor 9:8). "God is able." Hannah returned to her desk. She opened her veins. The cursor did not mock her—"God is able."

Prophetic ministry is a continual challenge. The challenge is not new or stronger today because "times have changed." Proclamation has always been difficult and demanding. Think about Moses. "I can't speak. They won't believe. Who am I? Who are you?" (Exod 3). Think about Isaiah. "I am lost, for I am a man of unclean lips . . . all flesh is grass . . ." (Isa 6). Think about Paul's advice to Timothy. "Proclaim the message; *be persistent* whether the time is favorable or unfavorable, convince, rebuke, encourage, with the *utmost patience* in teaching" (2 Tim 4:2; emphasis mine). Prophetic imagination is always challenging.

Craig Dykstra insists that preachers have a unique opportunity to notice and understand things that others cannot or do not notice or understand. "Life lived long enough and fully enough in the pastoral office," he observes, "gives rise to a way of seeing in depth and of creating new realities that is an indispensable gift to the church, to all who are members of it, and indeed to public life and to the world."[5] "Seeing in depth," or "noticing" is a feature of wonder. Dykstra names it "overwhelming."

What "overwhelms" you? We usually think of that word in negative terms. We're overwhelmed when we have more tasks than time or when there are more bills than money. Like Hannah, we can be overwhelmed when words are hard to find or when complex problems emerge and solutions are few.

When we're overwhelmed we feel like we're drowning, which perfectly suits the word's origins. *Whelmn* means to submerge completely. In early usage, *whelm* meant to turn upside down, to overthrow. That sounds about right. When we are overwhelmed we are turned upside down, we are

5. Dykstra, "Imagination and the Pastoral Life," 27.

buried, crushed, overpowered. That can happen to prophetic imagination. It can be crushed by something as simple as a busy schedule or more darkly by the fear of failure or fear of saying the wrong thing or saying the right thing and losing friends. Prophetic imagination can be buried because we don't want to offend or upset or because we lack courage to "get up" and follow where Christ leads. We may hear "the voice over the waters" but it is silenced because we find it safer to keep our mouth shut or because dreaming kingdom dreams can be costly.

Prophetic imagination can be crushed, buried, but, as Dykstra points out, there's another side of being "overwhelmed." We can be overwhelmed by the beauty of a sunset, by the birth of a child, by unexpected generosity, or more pointedly, as Dykstra writes, we can be overwhelmed by the "the buoyancy of God . . . in life and in death—we are upheld by God's own everlasting arms."[6]

How do we hold on to "buoyancy"? How do we stay afloat? Reading helps, as does study, rest, play, friendship, worship—all of these keep us from sinking in the deep end. I try to practice these things, as I imagine you do. I care for my soul and my body, but I find that I stay afloat best when I relax and let go of my need to be in control, to be in charge, to be right, to be first. I stay afloat best when I am overwhelmed by the awesome mystery of the triune God whose power is made perfect in our weakness (2 Cor 12:9). When we are overwhelmed by the beauty, goodness, and mercy of God, we are free to preach the good news of Jesus Christ.

Priest

Midway through his funeral homily Graham lost his voice. Graham always lost his voice when he wept. And that day he wept. Graham was surprised by his tears. He didn't know Charles very well. Charles and his wife, Alice, were relatively new members. They were regulars in worship and in the class Graham taught on Sunday mornings. Charles always had good things to say in class, though some days he fought for his words due to a stroke three years earlier. Graham admired the tenacity in Charles and his good humor despite disabilities. Maybe that prompted Graham's tears or maybe it was the way the fifty-six-year-old had died—suddenly, unexpectedly.

Charles had been rushed to the hospital and admitted to the ICU with an unexplained high fever. When Graham saw him around six that night

6. Ibid.

he was sitting up in bed and feeling much better. After they prayed, Charles thanked Graham for coming by and talked about the possibility of going home the next day. Charles smiled broadly as Graham left the room. Maybe that brought the tears at the funeral—the happiness and hope Charles displayed the last time he had seen him alive. Five hours after Graham had visited Charles, Alice phoned, "Charles is dead." Graham went straight to the hospital. When he saw Alice in the ICU she was standing in the doorway to Charles's room. "It happened so fast. One minute he was fine and the next he was gone." Maybe that brought the tears—the memory of Alice's shock and disbelief, the emptiness and silence of death, in a once noisy ICU.

Ministers are privileged to be present at the best of times and at the worst of times in the lives of their people, God's people. We are likely among the first called not only when there's a death but also a birth. We get to baptize babies, confirm youth, and walk with newly born disciples. When marriage is proposed, again we're among the first to know. "Is the church available, are you available?" But there's more than logistics; we listen and counsel as two lives become one. At so many beginnings, we get to celebrate, dance, and drink deeply from the wellspring of common life.

"Rejoice with those who rejoice, and weep with those who weep" (Rom 12:15). The priestly office we hold locates us at the threshold not only of beginnings but also endings. To borrow an image from Michael Jinkins, we are "docents in the House of Wonder."[7] Docents, as Jinkins observes, help turn tourists into pilgrims[8] and for that we must walk with others not only during their beginnings but also their endings, the most obvious of which is death itself. But there are other deaths—divorce, broken relationships within and sometimes between families, unemployment, underemployment, substance abuse, mental illness, dementia, accidents, relocation, retirement, aging, failing health. The list goes on and on.

Priests are called when there's no one else to call, when there is no other help. Priests stand in-between. We intercede. And we do so because "while we do not know how to pray as we ought . . . the Spirit intercedes [for us and with us] with sighs too deep for words" (Rom 8:27). We can stand in-between because "Christ did not enter a sanctuary made by human hands, a mere copy of the true one, but he entered into heaven itself, now to appear in the presence of God on our behalf" (Heb 9:24). Docents remain resilient, weeping with those who weep and rejoicing with those

---

7. Jinkins, *The Church Transforming*, 83.
8. Ibid, 85.

who rejoice, because they know they are not the Light. We are witnesses to the Light. We testify to the Light, to the One who "in the days of his flesh, offered up prayers and supplications, with loud cries and tears . . . and was heard" (Heb 5:7). Priests intercede through the One who is heard.

Pastor

Rachael arrived at her office around 8 a.m. The part-time church secretary wouldn't be in for another hour. Rachael started her days by writing in her journal, praying, and reading Scripture. By the time the secretary arrived she was deep into a commentary and thinking about her sermon. After making a few phone calls and taking some, and after a dozen or so emails and texts, Rachael left the office and met over lunch with the church treasurer. Rachael never considered money management her strong suit, but she could read a balance sheet and over nine years had kept her 175-member, small-town church in the black.

Lunch brought no surprises. Rachael was relieved. The money was fine, not an over-abundance, but enough to get by. Rachael believed that was as it should be—daily bread.

Rachael left the diner and stopped by the nursing home to see Mrs. Blackmon. The ninety-year-old was feisty and a consumer of good books. Rachael always left Mrs. Blackmon feeling better than when she came. She imagined Mrs. Blackmon knew that. She was a real source of inspiration. The hour flew by. Energized by it, Rachael headed to the Williams. She had to make herself go.

The Williams never met a day they liked. When Rachael arrived the TV was set to a twenty-four-hour news channel—and loudly so—neither of the Williams heard very well. Rachel asked if they minded if the TV was off. Mr. Williams jabbed the clicker and launched into a tirade about the state of the economy. Mrs. Williams didn't see why the upcoming church homecoming couldn't be on Saturday rather than Sunday after worship. "It makes for a long day, you know? Some of us don't get around as well as we once did."

Secretly Rachael was thinking about how nice it would be if the Williams stayed home that day. Everybody would have a better time! But she kept that to herself. "Well, I have to go. I'm meeting with the choir director at four." Rachael prayed with the Williams and left thinking how sad it must

RESILIENCE: A CHRIST-SHAPED LIFE OF FREEDOM

be to sit in that dark house all day long with little more than the flickering blue light cast by a TV.

The meeting with the choir director went as all meetings with choir directors go. Hymns were chosen for the month, the liturgical calendar was reviewed—there were no fistfights, no broken bones. All in all, Rachael considered it a success.

The church board meeting was scheduled to start at 5:30 with soup and sandwiches. Twelve officers arrived, some looking exhausted from work; others refreshed having just come from the gym. The agenda that night was short, routine, and ended by seven. Rachael was glad for that. When the meeting ended, she turned out the lights and headed for home.

Pastors wear many hats and on any given day can expect a range of emotional switches. Emotional switching, adjusting our emotions to context, is taxing, tiring, and sometimes tricky. One moment we may be alone in the quiet of our study and the next we're throwing water balloons with the youth group. Switching requires emotional intelligence; it requires attending, noticing. It also requires imagination and daring, daring to imagine a life changed, daring to imagine new ways of being community, daring to imagine a church turned more fully toward the world, a church that is mission. Daring is inspired by the Spirit of God.

Pastoral leadership, in all its roles, prophet, priest, and pastor, is more art than science; it is more dance than technique. It is less about management and more about imagination. And imagination is grounded in wonder. As I said at the beginning of this book, wonder is not something we fabricate. Wonder is a response to the One who was crucified and is now risen. Don't wrap that too tightly. Don't try to tie it down. Don't hold it merely as an article of faith as if the crucified and risen Christ can be manipulated or explained. Rather, like the first disciples, keep walking with him. When we walk in wonder we are made resilient for a Christ-shaped life of freedom. When we walk in wonder we hold with joy and trembling fear the mystery of God. We are free to imagine, to dare and to dream. We are free to follow where Christ leads. And where Christ leads there is life.

For Reflection and Discussion

1. John Rae, Diana Nyad, and Ernest Shackleton are extraordinary examples of resiliency. When have you observed resiliency in others?

Name some examples. How would you describe the character of the resilient people you have known? What defined them?

2. "Get up and go." What in ministry gets you down? What takes the wind out of your sails? What frustrates you? Where does futility show up? More importantly, what do you do when you feel like you can't go on?

3. Sleeping in ministry—what does that look like for you? Have you ever had a "wake up call"? What changed about you? How did you do ministry differently as a result?

4. Moltmann insists that redemption is not only personal and social but also generational and cosmic. Do you ever worry that your frame of reference for ministry is too narrow? How might Moltmann's broader frame change how you imagine and do ministry?

5. What challenges your prophetic imagination? What nourishes, enlivens, enriches your prophetic imagination?

6. When was the last time you cried for someone in your congregation? When was the last time you rejoiced? Why are weeping and rejoicing necessary for ministry?

7. Name a time when you experienced an emotional switch. How does emotional switching affect you? How might attending to emotional switches shape the way you do ministry?

8. Do you agree that pastoral leadership is more art than science? Why or why not? Name some of the interfaces of art and science in your ministry. How does the interplay of technique and dance influence your ministry for a Christ-shaped life of freedom?

Bibliography

Barth, Karl. *The Doctrine of Creation: Church Dogmatics*, 3.1. Translated by J. W. Edwards, O. Bussey, and Harold Knight. Edinburgh: T. & T. Clark, 1958.
———. *The Epistle to the Romans*. Translated by Edwyn C. Hoskins. New York: Oxford University Press, 1977.
Bethge, Eberhard. *Dietrich Bonhoeffer: Man of Vision; Man of Courage*. Translated by Eric Mosbacher et al. New York: Harper and Row, 1970.
Bonhoeffer, Dietrich. *Letters and Papers from Prison*. Edited by Eberhard Bethge. New York: Macmillan, 1971.
Brown, Brené. "Listening to Shame." TED Talk, March 12, 2012.
Bryson, Bill. *A Short History of Nearly Everything*. New York: Broadway, 2003.
Collier, Paul. *The Bottom Billion: Why the Poorest Countries are Failing and What Can Be Done about It*. New York: Oxford University Press, 2007.
Dykstra, Craig, "Imagination and the Pastoral Life." *The Christian Century*, March 8, 2008, 26–31.
Friedman, Edwin. *A Failure of Nerve: Leadership in the Age of the Quick Fix*. New York: Seabury, 2007.
Frykholm, Amy. "Fit for Ministry." *The Christian Century*, October 31, 2012, 22–25.
Heifetz, Ronald A. *Leadership Without Easy Answers*. Cambridge, MA: Belknap, 2001.
Jinkins, Michael. *The Church Transforming: What's Next for the Reformed Project?* Louisville: Westminster John Knox, 2012.
Jung, Carl G. *Psychological Types*. Translated by H. G. Baynes. Princeton, NJ: Princeton University Press, 1976.
Kahneman, Daniel. *Thinking, Fast and Slow*. New York: Farrar, Straus and Giroux, 2011.
Keirsey, David, and Marilyn Bates. *Please Understand Me: Character and Temperament Types*. Del Mar, CA: Prometheus Nemesis, 1984.
Long, Thomas G. *What Shall We Say? Evil, Suffering, and the Crisis of Faith*. Grand Rapids: Eerdmans, 2011.
McGoogan, Ken. *Fatal Passage: The Untold Story of John Rae, the Arctic Adventurer Who Discovered the Fate of Franklin*. New York: Bantam, 2002.
Moltmann, Jürgen. *The Way of Jesus Christ: Christology in Messianic Dimensions*. Translated by Margaret Kohl. San Francisco: Harper Collins, 1990.
Mulder, John. "Pilgrim's Progress: You Can't Make It Alone." *Perspectives*, May 2010, 5–9.
Niebuhr, H. Richard. *Christ and Culture*. New York: Harper, 1951.

Office of the General Assembly of the Presbyterian Church (U.S.A.). *A Declaration of Faith*. Louisville: Office of the General Assembly of the Presbyterian Church (U.S.A.), 1977/1991.

Otto, Rudolf. *The Idea of the Holy: An Inquiry into the Non-rational Factor in the Idea of the Divine and Its Relation to the Rational*. Translated by John W. Harvey. London: Oxford University Press, 1958.

Polanyi, Michael. *Personal Knowledge: Towards a Post-Critical Philosophy*. Chicago: University of Chicago Press, 1962.

———. *The Tacit Dimension*. Chicago: University of Chicago Press, 2009.

Raines, Ben. "Ancient Underwater Forest off Alabama Coast is Much Older than Scientists Thought." *AL.com,* March 7, 2013. http://blog.al.com/wire/2013/03/ancient_underwater_forest_off.html.

Shackleton, Ernest. *South: The Endurance Expedition*. New York: Signet, 1999.

Taylor, Charles. *A Secular Age*. Cambridge, MA: Belknap, 2007.

Von Balthasar, Hans Urs. *Credo: Meditations on the Apostles' Creed*. New York: Crossroad, 1990.

Wikipedia. "Extinction." http://en.wikipedia.org/wiki/Extinction.

———. "Permian-Triassic Extinction Event." http://en.wikipedia.org/Permian-Triassic extinction event.

www.ingramcontent.com/pod-product-compliance
Lightning Source LLC
Chambersburg PA
CBHW032233080426
42735CB00008B/834